with love & gratitude
for our friendship...

X Diane

The sacred bathing places
are fine
for taking a bath.
But take Kabir's advice
and bathe at home.
It's cheaper.

And it's okay to go to shrines
and see the idols, graven images
and Shiva's lingam.
Some of them are beautiful art,
but they cannot speak to you,
or open the doorway to your heart.

The Koran and Upanishads are mere words.
Inspired words but only words.

What do you seek?
A clean body, a stone statue,
a hundred thousand words?
Or the One?
Listen!
His hiding place
is closer
than you think.

—KABIR, page 106

Other Books by William M. Stephens

Footprints in the Sand
Our World Underwater
Science Beneath the Sea
Southern Seashores
Islands
Come with Me to the Edge of the Sea
Life in the Open Sea
Answers on Aging
A Day in the Life of a Sandy Beach
Life in a Tidepool
Tennessee Public Benefits Law Manual

with Peggy Stephens:
Octopus Lives in the Ocean
Killer Whale
Sea Turtle Swims the Ocean
Hermit Crab Lives in a Shell
Sea Horse: a Fish in Armor
Flamingo: Bird of Flame

SOULS
ON
FIRE

William M. Stephens

Oceanic Press
Nashville • Cullowhee • Maui

Oceanic Press

©1998 by Oceanic Press
Nashville, Tennessee
Printed in the U.S.A.

ISBN #: 0-9658884-8-7
Library of Congress Card Catalog number 98-067303

CONTENTS

Foreword and Acknowledgments

Most of us have never seen a saint. Or if we have, we probably didn't know it. If you had met the young Francis Bernardone as he caroused at night in the streets of Assisi, would you have suspected he would someday become the best known saint in the Western world?

Suppose you heard that a beautiful woman in a brothel was actually a saint, and that her presence there was simply a cover for her work of saving souls? Would you take such a report seriously? Would any television or movie producer dare to tackle a story *that* far-fetched?

Or, let's say you were told that a practitioner of black magic, a mass murderer, was destined to become the most famous saint in all of Tibet. Would you think that could possibly be true?

Although the above examples are extraordinary, albeit true, they simply show that God is capable of *anything,* and God's love is always available to flow to any and all persons who sincerely ask for it.

God is infinitely creative, and so each saint is a unique individual, a copy of none, and one who can never be replicated. At the same time, it appears to be true that saints have some traits in common. They seem to radiate an aura of something very special. They stand out in a crowd. They have a sense of peace, love, joy, or good will that inspires confidence and acts as a kind of magnet. They have the ability to bring out the best in others. They seem not to be hampered by the traits of selfishness, lust, ambition, greed or anger.

I have been blessed to know a small group of men and women who exhibit many of those rare characteristics. They live in a spiritual community in India which I have visited many times over the past three decades. These dear friends would laugh at the idea that they behave in a saintly way. And they don't, of course, in any conscious sense. They simply are being themselves. They are full of joy and laughter, and they enjoy good food, practical jokes and funny stories. They are like the favorite aunts and uncles most of us would like to have.

One of them in particular, Eruch Jessawala, who served as right-hand man for thirty years to Meher Baba, first inspired my interest in researching and writing about saints, masters and mystics. Thank you, dear Eruch, for your patience, your prodigious memory, your love and your marvelous stories. My thanks, too, to all the other wonderful souls who served, and still serve, as members of Meher Baba's close disciples–his *mandali*.

Sincere thanks also to an eminently readable and open-minded magazine, *Fellowship in Prayer*, which has published articles written by me about Meher Baba, Rabia, Mirabai, Ramakrishna, Milarepa and other spiritual greats. In 1984, *Fellowship in Prayer* awarded me a grant that allowed me to travel to India to do research for this book.

Heartfelt thanks go also to my dear wife Peggy, whose loving support and editing skills have always been and still are indispensable to all of my work. I am grateful to Rusty Rust for the striking color photograph of a living flame used on the cover, and to Julie Rust for design and layout.

In writing these sketches about great souls and their fascinating lives, I have attempted to show their human qualities (after all, their inner lives are known only to God). I have tried to be factual, but not scholarly, and to use common sense in trying to separate legend from history. In the case of some of the subjects, there is a wealth of both objective and subjective material available. In the case of others, there is very little.

Putting words in the mouths of long-dead persons is a delicate and controversial matter. Most of these people spoke languages that are foreign to most readers of this book. So we must consider the loss or change in meaning brought about by even the best translations. Also, how well does idiomatic terminology convert to a foreign tongue? At the same time, we know that characters come to life more vividly when we hear them speak in our own (sometimes colloquial) language. While all languages and slang expressions change over time, the yearnings and other heart qualities of men and women remain much the same today as in Tibet or Iraq a thousand years ago.

An exciting trend today is to bring historical figures and their creative works into current colloquial language in an effort to make them more alive and easier to understand. This has been done with great success in the case of some mystical poets of Persia and India. If you haven't already done so, you might read the sparkling versions of the poetry of Rumi and Kabir that Coleman Barks and Robert Bly have given us. Look at the creative renderings of the poems of the immortal Hafiz that Daniel Ladinsky has produced. These are new *interpretations,* not new translations, and they are marvelous. The same principles apply to prose as to poetry. It is practical, I believe, to do *prose* renderings of what *could* have been the dialogue of persons who lived many centuries ago, and I have employed this device in some of the stories.

I first heard of Rabia, Mirabai, Babajan, Hafiz, Rumi, Kabir and Ramakrishna through Meher Baba and his disciples. Since I was an agnostic before I was first contacted (inwardly) by Meher Baba, I must give Baba, my Spiritual Master, full credit for this book. And even though some of the saints treated herein—for example, Francis of Assisi and Teresa of Avila—have been well known in America for centuries, I had no great interest in them until I learned that Meher Baba loved them dearly and even traveled to their tombs during the 1930s.

Some of the incidents in my account of the life of

Rabia, the eighth century Muslim saint, have rarely been published before. This is because Meher Baba, during the twentieth century, revealed fascinating facts about Rabia that do not appear in the historical literature. I refer specifically to her life in a brothel in the city of Basra. These facts about the saint first appeared in *The Meher Baba Journal* during the early 1940s. Most of the material about the life of Hazrat Babajan, the female Perfect Master who kissed Merwan Irani on the forehead and thereby unveiled his true identity, also came from articles that were published in *The Meher Baba Journal*.

I have received information, inspiration and guidance from Bhau Kalchuri's monumental (twelve volumes or more and still going) biography *Lord Meher*, and also from the six volumes (to date) of Bal Natu's wonderful set, *Glimpses of the God-Man Meher Baba*. Special thanks, also, to Don Stevens, Kendra Crossen and Ward Parks for their critical reading of my manuscript and their helpful comments and criticism.

I am grateful to the Chairman of the Avatar Meher Baba Perpetual Public Charitable Trust in Ahmednagar, India, for the use of Meher Baba quotations to which the Trust holds copyright. My gratitude also goes to Sheriar Press, Inc., and Sheriar Foundation, Myrtle Beach, South Carolina, and to Sufism Reoriented, Walnut Creek, California, for their many fine publications that have informed and inspired me for decades. Thanks also to Bill Le Page, Meher House Publications, Sydney, Australia, for his fine collections of delightful stories, and for his permission to use Meher Baba's story about Rabia that was told by Eruch Jessawala in Mandali Hall. Thanks also to Naosherwan Anzar, publisher, *Glow International* and author and editor of many outstanding books for his encouragement and friendship.

My treatment of Hafiz, who was Meher Baba's

favorite poet, leans heavily on the work of Paul Smith, whose remarkable *Divan of Hafiz* is the first biography and collection of the works of Hafiz to acknowledge properly the poet's spiritual status and to include brief comments on Hafiz from Meher Baba's book *God Speaks*. Also, with heartfelt appreciation for his creative renderings of Hafiz, I thank Dan Ladinsky for his counsel and advice, and for his permission to use several Hafiz renderings from his lovely book *The Subject Tonight Is Love*.

I received much inspiration and direct assistance from many other books listed in my bibliography. In particular, my article about that wonderful, courageous and unique soul George Fox could never have been written without relying heavily on the marvelous biography, *The Story of George Fox,* by Rufus M. Jones.

In researching the life of the Buddhist saint, Jetsun Milarepa, there is only one reliable source available, so I humbly thank the great Tibetan scholar W.Y. Evans-Wentz for his spiritual masterpiece, *Tibet's Great Yogi Milarepa*.

For well-known Catholic saints such as Francis and Teresa, there are numerous sources. For Teresa, I relied heavily on her *Life*. For Francis, I thank Julien Green and his publisher Harper Collins for his fine book, *God's Fool*, and for use of his translation of Francis's great poem, "The Canticle of the Sun."

To me, the women and men described herein epitomize the ecstatic approach to God that is known in India as *bhakti* yoga. This is said to be the highest form of worship, in which the lover pursues the Beloved until he discovers that, all the time, the Beloved was ardently pursuing *him*. What heartrending joy! What bliss to find the Divine Beloved as one's own intimate Lover!

William M. Stephens
Meherlani, Maui, 2/25/98

A Note About Personal Pronouns

Almighty God, being infinite and omnipresent, is surely beyond all distinctions of sex and gender. We live in a world of duality, however, and our minds are limited. Therefore, we cannot comprehend a sexless being wholly without attributes. Most of us tend to think of God as either the Divine Mother or the Divine Father.

Actually, I am convinced that God is *both* the Divine Mother and the Divine Father, and is also *beyond* both. He/She shares the limited consciousness of each of us and is at the heart of every being, creature and object.

But the English language is most confining. In any discussion of God, it is difficult to avoid using one or more of the personal pronouns, He, She, Him, Her or It. If we try to be absolutely accurate and impartial, we might use expressions like "He or She," "Him or Her," or "Him, Her or It." But, before long, our sentences get so complex that nobody wants to read them.

Consequently, in this book, when a personal pronoun referring to the Deity is called for, I will use the masculine form. In making this decision, I am influenced by the fact that all incarnations of God that are widely accepted—Zoroaster, Rama, Krishna, Buddha, Jesus Christ and Mohammed—appeared on earth in a male form. And, the contemporary spiritual master Meher Baba, whom many people accept as the most recent descent of God into human form, also came in a male form. We should note, however, that Meher Baba told his followers that, in this incarnation, he was functioning both as the Divine Mother and the Divine Father.

The High Road to God

God is in every religion, like the thread
through a string of pearls. Wherever you
see extraordinary holiness and power raising
and purifying humanity, know that God is there.
—**Bhagavad Gita**

In India a spiritual teacher was telling his followers about the "high road to God"—the way of love and surrender and of thinking constantly of God in the midst of everyday activities.

"But, Bhagvan," a disciple said, "how can I keep my mind on God when the monsoon is late, my crops are wilting in the sun, and the well is running dry?"

His guru nodded toward some women who walked gracefully along the dusty road, each with a brass pitcher atop her head. "That is how you should live in the world," he said. "They are gossiping and laughing, but a part of their minds is always aware of the pitcher. They maintain perfect balance as they walk, and they never spill a drop."

The teacher added, "In the same manner, you should keep God always in your mind. Before going to sleep at night, let your last thought be of God; and let your first thought on awakening be of God. The more you think about God, the more you will learn to love Him, because He is Love."

Of course, all religions tell us to love God. But loving God is not a simple thing. How do we love that awful force that spits fire from volcanoes and swallows great chunks of real estate in earthquakes and storms? How do we love an Infinite Being who gives birth to thousands of

infants a day, and also allows vast numbers to die from
catastrophes, disease and senseless violence?

Yet sacred books and spiritual teachers tell us that
God is Love. And, indeed, down through the ages, a few
great souls have shown us by their lives that the mere
process of falling in love with God can lead to great joy,
illumination and even ecstasy.

If we actually fall in love with God, we are told,
God reciprocates in kind. Since God is infinite, He can
give each of us His undivided attention. Not only does He
accept our love, He raises it to an infinitely higher level.
So, at such time as we demonstrate, through *our* love, that
we are ready to receive *His*, each of us becomes, in effect,
the Divine Beloved's one true lover. This lover-Beloved
relationship has been called "The Divine Romance."

An intimate, lasting relationship built on love and
trust doesn't develop overnight, of course. Infatuation may
come in a flash, but love must incubate and develop and
mellow with time. This is just as true of a relationship with
God as with a wholly human affair of the heart. It might
not begin with bells and whistles, or with any other sign to
indicate that the most important episode of your entire life
(or of your many lives) has just begun.

It may start when a person becomes very interested
in some spiritual figure such as Jesus Christ, Mohammed
or Krishna. Suppose you are moved to tears by a book you
read about Jesus, and the feeling persists for days and
weeks after you finish the book. Depending upon your
individual tendencies, you may search for more books on
Jesus; or you may seek answers from a minister, priest or
friend. Perhaps you will join a Bible study group.

As time goes on, if your interest in Jesus continues
to grow, you may develop an intimate, secret relationship
with Him. You may spend private time with Him each day
in a special place surrounded by pictures or mementoes
that have special meaning for you. Perhaps you will grow

to think of Him as your own personal Beloved, with whom you yearn to be united forever.

Perhaps you now keep pictures, books, and Bible quotes at various spots in your office and home to remind you constantly of Jesus. You may be moved to meditate for a period each day, or you may silently repeat the Jesus Prayer (or just His name) for hours at a stretch. The time may come when you decide to take a pilgrimage to some sacred place connected with His life. As time goes on, your love will blossom and grow and pervade your entire being, and you will feel greater joy than you ever dreamed possible.

This is what seekers, mystics and other true lovers of God have told us. You will meet some of them in the following pages, and you may find other persons in your daily life who possess some of the same heart qualities as these remarkable souls.

The belief that God is closer to us than our own breath; that He is within us and around us and loves us more than we could ever love anybody or anything, is at the heart of all religious faiths. Yet many religious people today do not take such beliefs seriously. They blame their fears and their hopelessness on various problems outside themselves–the government, foreign nations, terrorist groups, crime, the millenium, the environment, or aliens from outer space. They seem to believe that God is impotent, ignorant of what is going on, or uncaring.

In general, people who consider themselves to be religious tend to associate God primarily with places of worship, such as churches, temples, synagogues, mosques and shrines; with congregations of worshippers; and with priests, preachers, rabbis, saints, nuns and monks. They contact God by going to church, participating in spiritual hymns, prayers, rituals and ceremonies, and by reading sacred texts. Many seem to believe that God can be approached only at special times and places, or through an

intermediary. They may complain about the godless state
of our educational institutions, and their cars may bear
bumper stickers proclaiming messages such as OUR
CHILDREN NEED TO PRAY. Although they profess to
believe in God, they do not really take God seriously.
They are afraid that God may have less power than our
armed forces, or the President, or China or Iraq. They take
the world seriously and God lightly.

There are, and always have been *some* people who
take God seriously (and the world lightly), who believe
that God is in charge, and that everything happens in
accordance with His will and His timetable. They believe
that real prayer is a private matter–a personal communion
or intimate conversation with the One who is our constant
companion–and that the lines of communication are
always open. They know from experience that God is
accessible on many levels and may be approached in a
multitude of ways–in a traditional place of worship, in the
natural cathedral of a forest; through a turning inward or a
reaching out; by looking into the eyes of a hungry soul, or
by sinking into the silence of one's own heart.

In the following pages we will explore the time-
honored personal approach to God as practiced by a dozen
great souls from both East and West. These seekers of
Truth, often in defiance of tradition and convention,
carved their own individual paths through the thorny maze
of creation in a quest for union with the Almighty. Such
spiritual giants have appeared in every land, heritage and
faith; but more are known, perhaps, from India, where the
heterogeneity of Hinduism permits a totally unstructured
approach to God. In the East, the path of *bhakti* (love and
devotion) has been recognized for many centuries as a
special form of yoga. Not only Hindus, but Jains, Sikhs,
Parsees, Buddhists, Muslims, and some Christians
recognize bhakti as a path to God.

More than two thousand years ago, a bhakti-like

movement rose in Persia in reaction to the rigidity of the ancient religion of Zoroastrianism. (Religions, like some people, tend to become lethargic and dogmatic in old age, and may finally succumb to heart failure.) This movement, which later became known as Sufism, was fanned into passionate flame by the persecutions of Islam. Orthodox Muslims, to whom any form of identification with God is heretical, devised unspeakable tortures for Sufis who dared to suggest that God could become man, or man become God.

Consequently the Sufi masters often disguised their teachings with symbols of dissipation, eroticism and skepticism. Atheists and profligates were safe from persecution, but the dervish who asserted that God was within his own heart might be skinned or buried alive. (Centuries later, in England, George Fox and his followers were beaten and imprisoned for much the same reasons. But Fox used plain language and not mystical poetry to denounce the hypocrisy of his tormentors.)

In the Sufi poetry of Attar, Rumi, Hafiz, Omar Khayyam and others, wine was the symbol for divine love. The wine-merchant (*Saki*) was the spiritual master who fills the cup within the heart. Images of drunkenness refer to the God-intoxication of the whirling dervishes, whose ecstatic dance symbolizes the dispensation of grace by the Lord. As the dervish whirls, his raised right hand receives the showering grace from above, which is sown on the earth by his left hand.

The land of Persia is said to have produced more sublime poetry than the rest of the world combined. Undoubtedly the "golden age" of Persian poetry was stimulated by the presence of many great poets who were also great lovers of God. Attar, Rumi and Hafiz are all recognized by Sufis as having achieved the highest spiritual status–that of a Qutub, or Perfect Master, one who has attained union with God while still inhabiting a human

body. If we accept the high spiritual status of such poets, it
is easy to ascribe hidden meanings to such "light verse" as
these lines by Hafiz:

All my pleasure is to sip
Wine from my Beloved's lip.
I have gained the utmost bliss--
God alone be praised for this.

During the fourteenth century, Hafiz perfected a
kind of song-poem known as the *ghazal* (pronounced
"guzzel"), which is still popular throughout India and in
Middle Eastern areas where it has not been suppressed by
Muslim fundamentalists. The above fragment and the one
below are from translations by A.J. Arberry.

Saki, the dawn is breaking:
Fill up the glass with wine.
Heaven's wheel no delay is making–
Haste, haste, while the day is thine!
. . .
When Fate on his wheel is moulding
Jars from this clay of mine,
Let this be the cup thou'rt holding
And fill up my head with wine!

The bhakti poets of India carried the lover-Beloved
symbology even farther. The Divine Beloved (often seen
in the man-form of Krishna or Shiva) is treated as the
reluctant bridegroom who must be entreated, cajoled or
seduced. The aspirant is the bride who, feverish with
desire, seeks to be ravished and utterly consumed by the
Lord. Just as some Catholic nuns wear a wedding band
and considered themselves to be espoused to Christ, the
devotee considers his or her only true union to be with
God. Shaivite poets write of cuckolding their lawful

spouse by sleeping with the Lord. By representing the desired union as unlawful, more obstructions are seen in its accomplishment, and the passion for consummation is thereby intensified.

Becoming God's Bride

Aspirants of either sex may think of themselves as God's bride. God is the only male force in creation, they hold, and we are all women before Him. Some aspirants, on the other hand, worship God as the Divine Mother. In either case, the goal of life is to surrender to the Beloved all the love and desire we feel for the opposite sex. In return, God purifies and spiritualizes the lust we direct to Him. By receiving our passions for the flesh, God draws us closer to perfection. As Swami Vivekananda wrote:

Let all our passions and emotions go to Him.
They are meant for Him, for if they miss their mark
and go lower, they become vile. When they go straight
to the Lord, even the lowest of them becomes
transfigured. All the energies of the human body
and mind must have the Lord as their one goal.
All loves and passions of the heart must go to God.
He is the Beloved. Whom else can the heart love?
He is the most beautiful, the most sublime.
He is beauty itself, sublimity itself. Who in
this universe is more fit to be the husband than He?
So let Him be the husband. Let Him be the Beloved.

To many of us in the West, the view expressed by Vivekananda seems strange and even unnatural. The lover-Beloved paradigm has almost disappeared from the Western religious tradition. The concept is foreign to most Protestants and has been forgotten by most Catholics and Jews. In the past, however, Christianity produced many

saints, mystics and poets whose personal, fervent and
devoted approach to God was indistinguishable from that
of the Sufis and bhaktas. And, going back farther, we find
the lover-Beloved passion described vividly in the Old
Testament. In the Song of Solomon, we read:

I sleep, but my heart waketh:
it is the voice of my beloved that knocketh. . .
I opened to my beloved; but my beloved had withdrawn
himself, and was gone: my soul failed when he spake;
I sought him but could not find him; I called him,
but he gave me no answer. . . .
I charge you, O daughters of Jerusalem,
if ye find my beloved,
that ye tell him I am sick for love. ...

Those who walk the Path of Love are blessed by
frequent, if not continuous, companionship with the Lord.
Moved by inner promptings, their guiding genius is the
divine fire within—the indwelling God. Their paths lead
through the heart primarily, as opposed to the head.
Ultimately, the Path of Love brings about a perfect balance
of the head and heart, allowing one to accomplish all
worldly tasks with the head and hands while the heart
remains centered on God.

God, it seems, is more accessible to the heart than
to the intellect. The approach to God through the heart is
the way of joy, bliss and inner peace. It can produce the
kind of unconquerable courage displayed by countless
Christian and Sufi martyrs, and by such rare souls as
Francis of Assisi and George Fox of England. These two
lovers of God, though poles apart on the surface, were
fellow travelers on the Path of Love. Only the times,
places, politics and methods were different.

Obedience and surrender lie at the heart of the Path
of Love. We must, in the most complete sense possible,

give everything to the Divine Beloved, who rests at the center of our being. We surrender not only our will but our thoughts, aspirations and deeds, good and bad. Surrender itself includes the Lord's acceptance of our gifts. When we surrender, He responds and our hearts rejoice. As the Apostle Paul wrote: "The current of my life flows on swiftly . . . I live, yet not I."

The path through the heart has several stages, beginning with ritualistic worship and growing into constant remembrance of God, and, eventually, absorption in God. In describing the higher stages (*Para-Bhakti*), Avatar Meher Baba wrote: "... It is not necessary for you to stop carrying out your worldly duties and obligations to achieve or to practice this higher *Bhakti*. You may conduct your business or follow a profession; you may lead the family life and look after all your necessary external requirements; but amidst all your worldly engagements you should ever be alert on the Lord. The more you can remember the object of the heart-worship, along with the routine work of your everyday life, the closer you are to the Goal."

Ramakrishna, a nineteenth century *Sadguru* (Perfect Master), tells us that the Path of Love is not only the fastest and most direct path to God; it is also the easiest, since God does all the work. The aspirant must do only one thing: focus on God. "He has not to suppress any single one of his emotions," wrote Ramakrishna's leading disciple, Swami Vivekananda. "He only strives to intensify them and direct them to God."

No austerities, reading of scripture, or repentance?

None are prescribed or required, but they may well develop naturally as we surrender to the will of God. The important thing is, we don't need to concern ourselves with any kind of ritual, ceremony, discipline or diet. As we think about God more and more, our devotion increases. We change, and the world changes. We find ourselves giving up habits and traits that do not please our Beloved.

Nothing can be held back. As our love grows, God opens up every aspect of our being. Our relationships with family and friends change and expand. (Of course, some relationships cannot survive the fire of Love and must be broken off.) Our attitudes toward society and the world mature and become more perceptive.

Think about it. If you admired Hitler and thought of him constantly, you would soon start acting like your idol. You might take on all of his qualities, good and bad, that you admire. But if you think of the Christ constantly, you can only grow closer to perfection. You cannot assimilate evil qualities since Christ, as a manifestation of God on earth, was and is perfect.

On the Path of Love, we need never dwell on our faults or sins. All we need do is dwell on the Lord. The mighty attraction for God dims all other attractions, and our low desires gradually disappear. The love for God that grows in our heart leaves no room for anything else. In whatever we do, we express God's love. No longer enslaved by desires, we become totally free. Our will is God's will.

Meister Eckhart in one of his sermons quoted a saying of St. Augustine that man *is* what he loves. He added: "If he loves a stone, he is a stone. If he loves a human, he is a human. If he loves God—I dare not say more, for if I said that he would then *be* God, ye might stone me." [Meister Eckhart knew the Lord intimately. Consequently he was called on the carpet by his superiors in the Church on more than one occasion for allowing the truth he knew in his heart to escape through his lips.] In Luke 6:40, we read: "No disciple is above his Master, but everyone when he is perfected is *as* his Master."

Meher Baba uses the example of a train pulling a string of boxcars containing goods. The engine does all the work. All the cars have to do is hold on. It doesn't matter what they're hauling—whether it's gold, lumber or garbage. If the cars hold on, they are carried straight and true to the destination.

All we must do is hold to the Lord through thick and thin. If we allow Him to steer and to set the pace, He will carry us through the mountains, deserts, triumphs and crises that might otherwise confuse our sense of direction. But if we turn loose for even a moment, we may be in jeopardy. If we allow ourselves to make a decision, enter a business meeting, get involved in a new relationship while He is not at the center of our thoughts and hearts, we are apt to be confused or controlled by our own self-centered ego-mind instead of by His infallible Divine Wisdom.

The most important work we can do is to cling to our Beloved. As Meher Baba told his disciples, "Your business is to love God. The rest is His business."

By holding onto the Lord–by staying in the sweet, safe arms of the Divine Beloved–we are not only carried to the Goal in the fastest possible time; we are transformed along the way. On arriving at the final destination, we will realize that we and the object of our search are one and the same. During the journey from unconscious divinity to conscious divinity, the Lord removes the barriers of separation and makes us one with Him. Our limited ego is transformed into the unlimited, infinite ego of God.

The men and women we shall meet on this journey of the heart come from many countries and backgrounds. By birth, they were Hindu, Muslim, Christian, Buddhist or Zoroastrian. All had one quality in common–a love for God that exceeded all other loves, including the love of religion itself. Some of them (Fox, Kabir) could be said to have rejected all forms of organized religion that existed in their time and place. Others (Ramakrishna, Rumi, Hafiz, Meher Baba) could be said to have embraced (and transcended) all religions.

All of them lived during the past thirteen hundred

years–since the last previous manifestation of the God-man as Mohammed the Prophet. According to Meher Baba, earlier manifestations of the God-man include Jesus Christ, Buddha, Krishna, Rama and Zoroaster. After each advent of the God-man, the world has been blessed with a great renaissance of the heart and spirit.

"Avataric periods are like the spring-tide of creation," wrote Meher Baba. "They bring a new release of power, a new awakening of consciousness, a new experience of life–not merely for a few, but for all. Qualities of energy and awareness which had been used and enjoyed by only a few advanced souls are made available for all humanity. Life as a whole is geared to a new rate of energy."

Here, then, are some of God's favorite lovers–gifts left to us from His last "spring-tide of creation." In His infinite compassion, God has given us a few pearls from His Ocean of Love, so that we might enjoy their beauty, study their lives, and cherish their memory while we watch and experience the building force of God's new tidal wave, which has already begun to shake the earth.

Rabia of Basra
(717-801)

From slavery to brothel to sainthood

Dear God, whatever You have set aside for me of worldly
things, give to those who fear and reject You.
Whatever You have prepared for me in the next world,
give to Your friends and admirers.
For You, my Love, are all I want.

–a prayer of Rabia

In the latter part of the twentieth century, the city
of Basra, Iraq's only seaport, has been much in the news,
especially during the war with Iraq. But twelve and a half
centuries ago, Basra was best known for reasons that had
nothing to do with oil wells or air strikes. Basra was a
major trading center even then and was famous for its deli-
cious dates, which grew to perfection in the 120 degree
temperature.

Among residents of Basra in those days, their city
had a claim to fame that was too special, and too personal,
to be divulged to visitors except on a one-to-one basis.
The city of Basra was said to be the home of the most
beautiful woman in the world. Her name was Rabia, and
she lived in a brothel. People spoke of Rabia in hushed,
reverent voices, and outsiders seldom learned the special
secret behind Rabia's presence in such a place.

The secret was that Rabia was not only the epitome
of beauty; she was the soul of purity and grace. She was,
in fact, a saint.

These incredible facts of Rabia's life were revealed

in the twentieth century by Avatar Meher Baba to his close
disciples. Rabia was one of Meher Baba's favorite saints,
and one to whom he had a close connection. According to
Meher Baba, Rabia achieved God-realization in a later
lifetime (in the 19th century, in fact) as Babajan of Poona,
who is featured in a later chapter.

Rabia lived in a very difficult time in history, the
century following the life and death of Mohammed the
Prophet. Mohammed died in 632 A.D., and a period of
turmoil, upheaval and spiritual renewal came to the Arab
world. As the star of Islam rose over the Middle East, the
ancient religion of Zoroastrianism was on the wane. In
Persia, the followers of Zoroaster were being persecuted by
the militant Muslims, and many Zoroastrians fled to India
and Pakistan, where they established their identity as
Parsees. At the same time, mysticism was flowering in the
Persian Gulf region and would in time produce the greatest
poet-mystics the world has ever known–Attar, Rumi and
Hafiz, among others.

As in all periods of spiritual awakening, nature also
went on a rampage, bringing earthquakes, drought and
plagues. This was the world into which Rabia was born in
717 A.D.

Rabia means "fourth," and she was the fourth
daughter of a poverty-stricken family in Basra, which lies
near the confluence of the Tigris and Euphrates rivers,
where, according to Biblical scholars, the Garden of Eden
was located. Rabia was still a tiny child when both of her
parents died in a famine. The sisters became separated, and
Rabia wandered, hungry and homeless, until a peddler
seized her and sold her to a slave-trader.

Rabia's first slave-master was a tyrant who drove
her mercilessly. But Rabia, even as a girl, was sustained
by remarkable inner strength, and she accepted everything
that happened to her as the will of God. Despite the
harshness of her life, she radiated serenity and purity.

At the age of twelve, Rabia was returning from the fields with a pitcher of goat's milk on her head when a ruffian attacked her. Running into a gulley, she fell, spraining her wrist and spilling the milk. Seeing that escape was impossible, she inwardly called out for God's help and immediately felt His grace flow through her. In the silence of her heart she heard God say that He was always with her and would protect her.

She rose and calmly faced her assailant who, frightened by the strange light in the girl's eyes, ran away without harming her. When she returned home, her master flew into a rage and beat her for spilling the milk. Shortly after this, he sold her to a merchant.

Her new owner was more considerate than her old one, but he required her to do all the cleaning, cooking and errands for a large household. Her only time to herself was late at night when everyone else was asleep. One morning before dawn, the merchant woke to hear his slave's voice raised in prayer. Creeping toward the sound, he saw her kneeling in a tiny meditation space she had created. Above her head was a light that illuminated the room. Rabia was saying, "Dear Lord, you know I want to serve only You. Must I serve both You and a man?"

God removes her bonds of slavery

Shaken, the merchant returned to his bed. The next day he gave Rabia her freedom, and she walked into the desert seeking solitude with her Divine Beloved. For a time she lived alone in a cave, communing with God and playing her flute. When she needed food, she emerged to earn money playing her music.

Rabia grew to become a beautiful woman with luminous eyes and finely chiseled features. A brothel keeper who heard her music offered her a position at his establishment, and she accepted. He was sure that her unearthly beauty would attract many men, and in this he

was not disappointed. Men, indeed, were always drawn to
Rabia, but her only lover was God.

When traveling merchants heard that the world's
most beautiful woman was to be found in a Basra brothel,
they were naturally intrigued. Often, they could not rest
until they saw the woman. Whether they went merely to
see her, or with the intention of buying her favors, the
result was always much the same. They were so struck by
her pure countenance and inner glow that they fell at her
feet, sobbing, or they left in confusion and shame. Many
came for the sole purpose of feasting their eyes on her and
listening to her stories about God and God's love. Often
they left transformed.

Working in a brothel for the glory of God

Meher Baba told a beautiful story of Rabia's life in
the brothel, and how she touched men's lives through her
beauty and purity. Baba's close disciple Eruch Jessawala
related the story as follows:

In the days of Rabia, it so happens that a young
man from Shiraz, in Iran, comes to Basra on business. He
is interested in seeing all the sights, so he asks everyone
he meets about the special features of the city. They tell
him of their gardens, their groves of date palms, and their
fountains.

"Yes, yes," he replies, "I have been to many places
and I have seen such things. But is there anything really
special, or unique, about this place?"

After a pause, his informant says, "Yes, there is."

"What is it?"

"The most beautiful woman on earth."

The young man laughs. "There are many beautiful
women in Iran, too."

"But not like this one."

Still grinning, the visitor shrugs and departs. Later
he puts the same question to the manager of a store. The

shopkeeper thinks for a moment and then nods his head. "Yes," he replies. "There is a very special person here. A lady. You have never heard of her. She is called Rabia of Basra."

"Oh, is that so? Who is this Rabia of Basra, and what is so special about her?"

"She is one whose beauty surpasses all beauty."

"Is that a fact? Well, where would I go to see this beautiful Rabia?"

"She lives in a brothel."

"Ha!" The visitor rolls his eyes. "I've heard that story before. In Iran we have prostitutes, too."

"Oh, but this woman is different."

"That's what they all say!" Laughing, the young man goes on his way. But wherever he goes and asks questions, he hears the name "Rabia." He is not interested in finding a prostitute, but he is intrigued because there is never a trace of vulgarity in the remarks about the lovely woman. Yet the whole city seems awed by her beauty.

Finally he decides he must see her. He goes to the brothel, where he is greeted by a matron, who asks him what he wants.

He replies that he is a traveler from Iran, and he wants to see Rabia of Basra.

"Oh, I see. Are you prepared to pay the fee?"

"Yes, yes. I'll pay the fee. I have money."

"The fee is exorbitant."

"I don't mind. Whatever it costs."

He pays the fee and she takes him to a comfortable suite, where he takes a seat. He sees no one. After a while he walks about the room and notices, in a side room, a figure knelt in prayer. Her beauty takes his breath away. How could such a lovely, obviously spiritual lady be living in such a place as this? It would surely be a sin, he thinks, to touch her in a carnal way. At the same time, he is excited by her nearness and her overpowering presence, and he cannot take his eyes off her.

Finally she rises from her prayers and greets him with a gentle smile, and he feels an aching in his heart. Her voice is like music as she says, "I am sorry to keep you waiting. You must be hungry." She claps her hands, and her attendants come. "Bring our special feast for this gentleman. He is our guest tonight. Would you like a glass of wine? What kind of beverage do you prefer?"

"Oh, it doesn't matter. Anything," he says. He thinks: *It is good that she is not too absorbed in prayer. She offers me food and drink . . . and she certainly is as beautiful as they say!*

During the lavish meal, he opens up his heart and tells her all about himself. She listens carefully to his stories of his life and travels. As he talks, he drinks in her beauty. She asks him about his visit to Basra, and if he has seen all the sights.

He smiles. "Yes, and everywhere I went I was told of your beauty. That's why I'm here. I had to see you for myself."

"I'm glad you came. But after all, what is this beauty that people talk about? It is all a passing show. I will grow old and have wrinkles, just as you will."

And then she speaks of the love and beauty of God, and how God's beauty never fades but only grows and increases. "The goal of life is to love God and become His own," she says. The young man is enchanted by her lilting voice and her soulful eyes, and he hangs on every word as she talks on until the early hours of the morning. By that time, he is her devoted slave, and he has forgotten that he had harbored lustful desires for her.

With tears in his eyes he thanks her for the most wonderful evening he had ever spent. "If I can ever do anything for you, dear Rabia," he said, "please tell me."

She smiles. "I have one request."

"Just ask. Anything I have is yours. My wealth.

Anything you wish."

"Just one little thing is all I ask. Never tell anyone what you have heard here. Allow the people to come to me. This beauty is only a trap set for them. God has put me here for His purposes. Promise me you will never tell."

"Oh, I see!" he says. "That is the secret of this place. The whole city celebrates your beauty. Yet nobody told me the secret behind it."

She nods. "I extract the promise from everyone who comes. My beauty is my strength to fight in the cause of the Lord."

Her followers increase

The time came when Rabia's devotees built her a retreat on a hillside, and she left the brothel. With each passing year, the number of her followers increased.

One of her disciples was Hasan of Basra, who would also be recognized as a Sufi saint. Once Hasan was chided by a friend for being the disciple of a woman. Hasan shrugged and replied: "Would you believe that I spent an entire day and night with the beautiful Rabia, speaking of the Way and the Truth, and never once did it cross my mind that Rabia was a woman and I was a man?"

In the twelfth century, four hundred years after Rabia, the famous poet Attar wrote a book called *Memoirs of the Saints*, which is the oldest known Persian book about saints. To Attar we are indebted for many of the stories about Rabia.

Attar tells of a pilgrimage Rabia made to Mecca with only a donkey for company. While crossing the Arabian desert, the donkey collapsed and expired. Rabia removed her belongings from the animal's back and then knelt to pray. "Beloved God," she said, "You are calling me to You, but You have let my donkey die. I am alone in the wilderness. Tell me what You wish me to do."

The donkey stirred and slowly got to its feet. Rabia

repacked her things on the animal's back and continued on her way. As she neared Mecca, she saw a black cubical building coming to meet her. It was the sacred *Kaaba*, the Muslim holy of holies and the mystical center of the world of Islam. The Kaaba is believed to contain the famous black stone that the angel Gabriel is said to have given to Abraham.

Watching the Kaaba approach, Rabia said, "I am not interested in the *house* of the Lord. It is the Lord I want." Instantly the Kaaba retreated and disappeared.

She has no interest in money or marriage

During her long lifetime, Rabia had many suitors. A wealthy trader from Baghdad begged for her hand, offering to match her weight with gold and jewels. In answer to his letter of proposal, she wrote: "It does not please me that you would be my slave or would lavish your riches on me. I do not want to be distracted from God for a single moment."

To another suitor, she said, "My existence is in God, and I belong to Him alone. The marriage contract must be sought from Him, not from me."

Rabia accepted all pain and suffering as gifts from God. Once, while she was taking a stroll with one of her followers, her hand was torn by a thornbush and began to bleed, but she ignored it.

"Don't you feel the pain?" her companion asked.

"My concern," said Rabia, "is to accommodate myself to God's will. I am content with His plan for my life and my day, and I thank Him for each of His gifts, large and small, painful or pleasurable."

Once when she was ill with a high fever, a visitor suggested she ask God to bring the fever down. "Surely God will take this suffering away if you will ask Him."

Rabia smiled. "Who do you think has given me this suffering? Is it not God?"

"Well . . . yes."

"Should I ask God to change His plans . . . to do something contrary to His will?" She shook her head. "It is not good to presume that the Beloved does not know what is best for my soul."

Even after Rabia became widely known and was surrounded by disciples and other seekers, she never lost her simplicity or her total reliance on God. Once, when she had fasted for weeks, her servant, while preparing a meal, realized she had no onion. "May I go borrow an onion?" the servant asked.

"Many years ago," Rabia said, "I promised God I would never ask for anything except His presence. I can do very well without the onion."

A moment later, a bird passing over dropped an onion at Rabia's feet.

Attar tells of a time when Rabia was sitting by the Tigris River when her disciple Hasan approached. To impress his teacher, Hasan threw his prayer rug onto the surface of the water and leapt onto it, using his occult power to keep the rug afloat. "Join me, Rabia," he said. "God will keep us afloat."

Rabia shook her head sadly. "Oh, Hasan, is it necessary to make a show of the power God has given you?" Tossing her own prayer rug into the air, and rising to kneel on it high above his head, she said, "Come up here, Hasan, where people can see us." Hasan looked away, ashamed.

Returning to the ground, Rabia said, "What you did, Hasan, a fish can do. And what I did, a bird can do. The real work of lovers of God is far beyond such games of yogis and fakirs. Let us devote ourselves to the real work."

As Rabia grew older, she slept less and less, and she spent most of each night in prayer on the flat roof of her house. "My Lord," she would say, "the stars are

shining and the eyes of kings and beggars are closed. All
the people have shut their doors, and every lover is with
his beloved. And here I am, my Beloved, alone with You."

Rabia lived to the age of eighty-four, then passed
away quietly in the presence of a large group of followers.
Before she died, she embraced each one, and then, in her
sweet and still-vibrant voice, she said a final prayer:
"Beloved God, if I worship You from fear of hell, burn me
in hell. If I worship You from hope of Paradise, exclude
me from Paradise. But if I worship You for Your own sake,
then do not withhold Yourself from me."

Francis of Assisi
(1182 - 1226)

LORD, make me an instrument of Thy peace.
Where there is hatred, let me sow love;
Where there is injury, pardon;
Where there is doubt, faith;
Where there is despair, hope;
Where there is darkness, light;
And where there is sadness, joy.
O DIVINE MASTER, grant that I may not so much
*   seek to be consoled as to console;*
To be understood, as to understand;
To be loved, as to love.
For it is in giving that we receive,
It is in pardoning that we are pardoned,
And it is in dying that we are born into eternal life.

–Francis of Assisi

In Italy during the Middle Ages, every city was an armed fortress and every young man a soldier. The Church had never been stronger—nor so corrupt. The priesthood was a rich and honored profession, and almost a law unto itself. Lewd and drunken behavior was rampant in the population at large, and also among the priests and nuns. It was a time for saints—those marvelous and creative souls who often develop outside the religious structure, where revolutionaries are usually found. In time, of course (often after they are dead), the establishment comes to accept them, to embrace them, and perhaps to build a church or sect or order around their name. After decades and centuries pass, the world comes to believe that the

saint was nurtured and molded by his or her religion—
instead of the other way around.

Francis of Assisi was the exception to the rule, of
course, in that his greatness was recognized even by the
Church during his lifetime. At the same time, we must say
that Francis owed very little to the Church and everything
to God. When the Church wanted to make him a priest,
Francis humbly refused the honor. Jesus wasn't a priest
either, he might have said.

He was born in the ancient city of Assisi, which
perches on the lower slopes of Mount Subasio. His father
Pietro Bernardone was a wealthy merchant who sold
textiles all over Europe. The boy was born while his father
was away on a sales trip to France. Upon his return, Pietro
insisted that his new son, whom his mother had named
John, be called Francesco ("Frenchman"). And he was
known as Francesco, or Francis, all his life.

His mother Pica, who proudly claimed to come
from a long line of French noblemen, taught him to speak
French. In the church school he attended, he also learned
Latin, which in those days was still the official language
of priests and politicians. But Francis never learned to
read or write very well. Only a few of his writings are
preserved. Most of the words we have from Francis were
delivered orally and written down (either on the spot or
later from memory) by his followers.

Francis was a spirited child and a born leader. In
adolescence he fancied himself a troubadour and he
yearned to be a knight. As a young man he threw himself
with abandon into revelry, pranks, music, flirtations and
wine. At the same time, however, his heart was often
touched by the plight of the hungry and poor, of which
there were many in Assisi. On his nightly escapades with
other wealthy young men, he might toss a handful of coins
to a beggar or even give away an expensive cloak. In quiet
moments he mused over the ironies of life—that an entire

family of poor people could live for weeks on what he threw away in a single night.

In 1202 the city of Perugia declared war on Assisi, and all the young men, including Francis, girded for battle. The opposing forces met on a plain between the two cities, and the Assisians were soundly defeated. Francis and some of his friends were captured as prisoners of war and spent a year in captivity. During this time of deprivation and hardship, Francis was sustained by inner strength, and even joy, and spent much of his time joking and cheering up his fellow prisoners. He sang the French troubadour songs he'd learned from his mother and laughed about the great times they would all have when they got home again.

And, indeed, after they were released Francis and his friends wasted no time in resuming their life of gaiety and indulgences. In fact, Francis's dissipations (coming after a year of forced inactivity) wrecked his health and he fell gravely ill at the age of twenty-two.

For weeks his life hung in the balance, and after he finally improved physically he was troubled by deep depression. One day, still so weak that he needed a cane, he made his way out through the city gates to gaze upon the spectacular vista of Mount Subasio on his left and the Umbrian plain on his right. He had hoped that the view (which he had always loved) would revive his zest for life. Instead, he felt only emptiness and disgust with himself for what he was doing with his life.

Chivalry, humiliation, and change

A few months later, he was offered the chance to join a group of knights who were organizing to fight in the army of Pope Innocent III in southern Italy. Francis seized the opportunity with enthusiasm. He would ride as a volunteer, displaying the buckler of a page since he had not been knighted. (But that was only a matter of time, he thought.) Wildly elated over the prospect of becoming a

hero in the glorious Crusades, Francis purchased the most
resplendent armor available. But then, seeing a poor knight
who was ill-equipped, Francis gave his splendid armor and
lance to the knight in need and ordered for himself a more
modest outfit.

All Assisi was present, cheering and singing, when
the knights and their pages assembled at the city gates.
The women and girls embraced the warriors and wished
them godspeed. Francis was in his glory, and he saw himself returning in triumph, with a lovely bride as his trophy
of war. He confided to his friends that he felt he would
become a great prince. His heart surging with pride,
Francis rode away with the knights.

That evening, after they stopped and made camp,
Francis had one of those deep inner experiences that often
came to him at times of crisis to change the pattern of his
life. According to St. Bonaventure, who many years later
wrote a classic biography of Francis, God came to the
young man and told him he should return home and await
further instructions.

In any case, on the following day, when the knights
reached the city of Spoleto, Francis stopped and went no
farther, and the others went on without him. What he told
them is anybody's guess. All we know is that he rode back
to Assisi alone, to face the scorn and humiliation of his
friends and parents. We also know that the mission he had
abandoned was destined to end in disaster. Most of the
knights were killed.

From that time on, Francis spent a lot of time
alone, in deep thought and meditation. Often he prayed,
seeking guidance, for hours on end, in a cave near a grove
of olives. Sometimes he wandered in the fields and woods
and on the slopes of Subasio. He also made a pilgrimage
to Rome. At St. Peter's, he emptied his purse upon the
apostle's tomb, then changed clothes with a beggar and
spent a day learning what it was like to be hopeless,

helpless and hungry in a large city.

Back in Assisi, he took to spending much of his time with the poor and homeless. He gave them money or clothes and food from his mother's kitchen. Throughout his life Francis could not pass a beggar without giving him something.

As time went on, his parents' concern grew to dismay and, on his father's part, to barely suppressed rage. It was one thing for his son to squander his money on wine and boisterous living. That was understandable for a lad of high spirits. Keeping up with the young nobles was vital to maintain the prestige of the Bernardone name. But throwing away money on the dregs and parasites of society was quite another matter. That was inexcusable and would not be tolerated.

In an attempt to resolve his conflicting loyalties to his family and to God, Francis consulted the bishop, who was not much help. "You are going too far, Francesco," the bishop told him kindly. "It is not your job to solve the social problems of Assisi. Did not our Lord say that the poor are always with us? The Holy Bible tells us to honor our father and mother. When you disobey your father, you are disobeying God."

While tension at home increased, Francis also went through another kind of test. All his life he had been repelled and disgusted by disease and physical deformity. In particular he had a horror of leprosy. Despite his best intentions, he could not bring himself to face a leper at close range.

One day, while riding his horse in the country, he came upon a leper who stood squarely in his path looking at him. Reacting with horror, he wheeled about to return the way he had come. But something seized his heart and forced him to rein to a stop, overcome by revulsion for his own weakness. "Coward!" his mind seemed to taunt. "You want to embrace Lady Poverty and live the life of Christ,

but you cringe at the sight of suffering. You are a disgrace
to your Lord."

He squared his shoulders, got off his horse, and
forced himself to approach the leper, staring into his eyes.
He gave the poor man his money, then taking a deep
breath he bowed and kissed the rotten sores on the leper's
hands. As he did so, the leper's disfigured face seemed to
change, and for a moment Francis felt he was looking into
the eyes of his Beloved Christ. Sobbing with love and gratitude, he embraced the leper, then returned home, his heart
aflame with a joy beyond words.

His mission revealed

One of Francis's favorite places was the chapel of
St. Damian, which stood atop a hill with a panoramic view
of the Umbrian landscape. Seldom visited by Assisians,
the chapel had fallen into ruins. One day, while Francis
sat in the sanctuary, praying for guidance, a wood carving
depicting Jesus Christ hanging on the cross seemed to
come alive, and Francis's heart was filled with light and
bliss. Crying with joy, he said, "Help me do Your will,
Lord. Let Your will be known to me." And Jesus said,
speaking from the cross, "Francis, repair my church."

Francis, of course, in his utter simplicity and
humility, could never have dreamed that the Christ was
assigning him the task of repairing and restoring the
Catholic Church–of saving Christianity from ruin. He
assumed, quite naturally, that his job was to repair the
chapel of St. Damian, which he promptly set out to do.

By this time, his life at home had become almost
unbearable, so he decided to live at the chapel while doing
the repairs. He went home to gather his possessions and
took a quantity of cloth from his father's stocks. He rode
to the market at Foligno, where he sold everything,
including his horse, and walked back to St. Damian with a

purse full of money, with which he intended to buy nails
and hammers and saws and building materials.

A few days later his father, boiling with rage, came
looking for him. Francis hid in the forest, staying there for
weeks, fasting and praying for guidance. When he finally
came out, determined to face his father, his clothes hung
on his body and his sunken eyes peered from a gaunt face
surrounded by unkempt hair and a scraggly beard. As he
stumbled through the city gate and up the narrow lanes of
Assisi, a group of children shouted, "Pazzo, Pazzo!"
[Madman! Madman!] Others took up the call, and a crowd
was watching when Pietro Bernardone came outside his
house to see what was causing the commotion.

When Pietro saw that his own son was the cause of
the scorn and laughter, his fury knew no bounds. Seizing
Francis bodily, he dragged him into the house, where he
cursed and vilified him for hours, and then tied him up
and locked him in a closet. "You will stay there until you
learn respect and humility," he thundered, "and until I
decide whether to flog you in the public streets or throw
you to the wolves!"

Several days later, when Pietro left the house for a
business trip, Pica unlocked the closet and fed her hungry
son. (For this she was beaten by her enraged husband
when he returned.) After eating a good meal for the first
time in weeks, Francis gave his loving mother a long and
tearful embrace, then bade her farewell and returned to his
work at St. Damian.

Again his father came looking for him, but this
time somewhat softened after venting his spleen on his
unfortunate wife. Finding Francis in the chapel, Pietro
tried to reason with him. "Don't you realize you have
humiliated your papa in the eyes of all the city? Me—
Pietro Bernardone, the most respected merchant in Assisi!
The whole city is making jokes about my son, the pazzo.
You have dragged the family name through the mud, and

you do not even say you are sorry."

"If you remember, Papa," Francis said, "I left home in a peaceful manner, and you reacted with violence. I have done nothing to be sorry for."

Pietro tore his hair in frustration. "You really *are* a pazzo! How can you behave like this—after all I have done for you! I have given you everything you could have wished, and you repay me by taking cloth from my house and selling it." He glared. "All for your worthless beggar friends . . . yes?"

"The money is there on the window sill," said Francis. "I was going to use it to rebuild this chapel."

Pietro seized the money and put it in his pocket. "This place is not worth repairing. Assisi has enough chapels. Nobody ever comes here but tramps and robbers" —his voice broke—"and my pazzo son. Listen to your father, Francesco. I give you one more chance. Come home and behave like a true son of Pietro Bernardone. I will forgive and forget. Agreed?"

Francis shook his head firmly. "No, Papa. I am staying here until I finish rebuilding this chapel."

"You will *not* stay here! I will not permit you to live here, so close to Assisi, bearing the great name of Bernardone and behaving like an idiot. From this moment you are not my son. I disown you. I forbid you to live in this district—a constant reminder of the disgrace you have brought on my house." He threw out his chest and shook his fist. "I command you to leave this place, and this region, and never show your face in Assisi again."

"You are no longer my father, so you cannot give me orders," said Francis softly. "I take my orders from my Father in Heaven."

"I'll show you who can give orders!" Pietro roared. "I'll have you jailed, you thieving little pazzo, if you are not gone from this district by tomorrow morning!"

Pietro filed a complaint, seeking to have Francis

expelled from the region. Francis sent word to the court that, as a servant of God, he was not under the jurisdiction of civil authorities. The magistrates referred the case to the church tribunal, which ordered a hearing. It was a *cause celebre* in Assisi, and the cathedral was jammed.

Francis stands trial

After Pietro Bernardone had stated his case, the bishop turned to Francis. "I have heard no evidence, my son, to convince me that you should be banished from this diocese. On the other hand, your father has threatened to disinherit you. Under the circumstances, would it not be best to return all property in your possession that rightfully belongs to your father?"

Francis nodded. Stepping outside the room for a moment, he returned stark naked, holding his clothes in a neat roll which he presented to the bishop, along with his few remaining coins. Livid with rage, Pietro Bernardone seized the items and left the room while Francis put on an old mantle and boots offered by the bishop's gardener. Leaving the cathedral and the city, he ascended the slopes of Mount Subasio.

It was April and the mountain seemed to swell with the joy of new growth and new life. Trees were budding and the forest pulsed with the songs of birds. Squirrels and chipmunks probed for food in the soft earth left by the melting snow. Intoxicated by the fragrance of spring, Francis laughed and sang and thanked God for His many blessings. While singing at the top of his voice, he came upon a band of ruffians, who ripped off his mantle and boots and threw him into a snowdrift. Now bruised and cold, he continued on his way, thanking the Lord for allowing him to suffer for the glory of God.

At the Benedictine monastery he offered to work for food and clothes, but his offer was refused. In the trash outside the monastery he found an old discarded shirt, which he put on. He walked to the house of a friend in the village of Gubbio, where he received clothes and shelter and food for a few days. At his next stop, a leper hospital, he was accepted with warmth and love, so he remained there for a time, helping to feed and bathe the patients, entertaining them with his songs and speaking to them of God. Inspired and rejuvenated, he walked back to St. Damian and set about to rebuild the sanctuary.

From time to time he went to Assisi to beg for building materials. First he would sing hymns in the town square to draw a crowd. Then he would speak of his plans to restore St. Damian and solicit their help. "Give me one stone and you will have a reward," he said. "Give me two stones and you will receive a double reward." Many of the people thought he was mad, but others were moved by his sincerity and gave him stones and other supplies, which he accepted gratefully and hauled on his back to the chapel.

It wasn't long before all of Assisi was accustomed to the gentle and shabby hermit who walked the streets or begged food at the kitchens. His presence was a source of constant embarrassment to his father, who would flush with anger and curse his son whenever their paths crossed.

After completing the restoration of St. Damian, Francis set about to repair other abandoned chapels in the area. The second one was on the site of an ancient temple that, according to local legend, had been there since before the birth of Christ. In the fourth century, four pilgrims returning from the Holy Land settled there and built a church. Later St. Benedict acquired the property and named it Portiuncula (Little Portion). His monks built a monastery that was used by the Benedictine Order for more than six hundred years. Before Francis came along, the Benedictines had abandoned the site as indefensible against the threat of invading Saracens and moved to the Benedictine fortress on Mount Subasio.

Francis loved the spiritual atmosphere of the Portiuncula. While laying stone and mixing mortar, he meditated on the untold generations of seekers who had lived and prayed there before him. Their love for God permeated the entire place and was a constant source of inspiration for him. He hoped for nothing more than to spend the rest of his life there in solitude and prayer.

A priest from the Benedictine monastery came to Portiuncula from time to time to say mass. Such occasions always filled Francis with great joy. One day while the priest was saying mass, Francis received a very special gift from God. It seemed to him that the priest became the living Christ, who was speaking directly to Francis. "Wherever ye go, preach, saying, 'The Kingdom of God is at hand,'" he intoned. "Heal the sick, cleanse the lepers, cast out devils. Freely ye have received, freely give. Provide neither silver nor gold nor brass in your purse, neither scrip nor two coats, nor shoes nor staff, for the laborer is worthy of his meat."

Getting down to essentials

That very day, Francis discarded his staff, writing paper, purse, and sandals, and made a decision to observe to the letter the precepts given to him from the Gospels. Each morning he walked barefoot to Assisi and preached a sermon in the streets. At first few people listened, but as time passed more and more came to hear his message about the peace and joy of following in the footsteps of Christ.

It is interesting to consider that Francis may have been the first Christian evangelist in the modern sense of the word. Before Francis came along, priests did not really communicate, in the true sense of the word. They lectured, harangued, and displayed their learning and piety. In public, they spoke only in Latin, a language that few

ordinary people knew, and they gave stilted, pedantic
monologues. Francis was the first to speak in the language
of the people—as Christ had done.

His first converts

One day, to his great joy, Francis attracted his first
two converts. First, a prominent and wealthy man of
Assisi, Bernardo di Quintavalle, approached the young
preacher and said he wanted to give his possessions away
and join Francis at the Portiuncula. While they were
talking, a second man, a lawyer named Pietro, came up
and said he too wanted to leave the world and join Francis.
The three of them prayed together and established the rule
of their order—that they would possess nothing and would
rely wholly and solely on God for their needs.

The first task of the three companions was to
distribute Bernardo's wealth to the poor, which caused a
great stir in Assisi. That done, they went to Portiuncula
and built lean-tos of limbs for the new arrivals, exactly
like the one where Francis slept. Then Bernardo and
Pietro made themselves cross-shaped tunics like Francis's.
About that time, they were joined by a fourth renunciate, a
farmer who became known as Brother Giles. Then came
an old priest named Sylvester who, only days before, had
fought greedily to grab double-handfuls of Bernardo's
money when it was passed out in the streets.

The five companions (who dubbed themselves the
Brothers Minor) started walking barefoot to neighboring
towns—usually in pairs—preaching of the love and peace
of God. At first they were ignored or insulted by most
villagers, and few housewives would give them even a
scrap of bread. But gradually people warmed up as they
realized that these men were poor by choice and were
clearly sincere.

And now, as three more men joined them, they

began to meet resistance from the Church itself. It was one thing for a lone man—the charming and disarming Francis—to beg each day for the glory of God. But for a whole crew of able-bodied men to live without jobs or possessions and to expect public support was quite another matter. Where would it all end? What would happen to the Catholic Church (which also relied on public support) and the business community if more and more prominent citizens (even priests!) left their homes and responsibilities to become barefoot vagabonds?

But the brothers were never idle. They nursed and fed the lepers, and they often earned their bread and beans by laboring in the fields. After begging in Assisi became difficult and unproductive, they planted their own gardens of vegetables, fruits, and flowers. (The only luxury Francis allowed was flowers.) While some of the brothers stayed home to tend the gardens and to work in menial jobs (in return for food and clothing only, since they never touched money), others ranged far afield.

Wherever they went, they greeted people with the words, "The Lord give thee peace." They were laughed at, harassed, and even assaulted, but they persisted cheerfully, never striking back or losing their tempers. Consequently more and more villagers were impressed by them. Now and then, a man would ask if he could join them, so their ranks slowly grew.

One day Francis and a companion were crossing the mountains north of Assisi. Francis was troubled at heart, and he yearned to be alone with God. Leaving his companion, he went up into the silence of the lonely peaks and, for hours, poured out his soul to God. And God responded, as He always responds to unconditional love. Suffused with light and bliss, Francis received a vision of multitudes of penitents coming to join his movement. When he came down the mountain, Francis was radiant but uncommunicative.

They returned to Portiuncula and, by one of those
"coincidences" that happen to people who are close to
God, all of the brothers returned home at about the same
time. Francis told of his experience on the mountain and
announced that they would go to Rome to seek the Pope's
official blessing for their order and their way of life.

Off to see the Pope
So the brothers, now twelve of them, undertook the
long walk to the center of Christendom, the Vatican. And,
astonishingly, they did see the Pope, who at first was cool
to the ragged little man who asked only to be allowed to
follow literally the precepts of Christ. Later, though, after
Pope Innocent III had a dream in which he saw Francis
literally holding up the walls of the Vatican, he gave the
Brothers Minor a limited commission. They were allowed
to preach penance and to exhort others to love God and
forsake evil; but they could not expound the dogmas of the
Church. Which was perhaps a blessing. They could keep
their focus on the love and mercy of Jesus Christ, which
was what Francis wanted.
Jubilant over their success, they returned to Assisi
and lived for a time in an abandoned building in a wooded
area of caves and waterfalls. After some months, the abbot
of the Benedictine monastery offered to deed the entire
Portiuncula property to the new order. Francis refused on
the ground that owning property was contrary to their
vows of poverty. But after the abbot offered to lease the
property to the Brothers Minor in return for an annual fee
of one basket of fish caught from the river, he readily
agreed. So God had given to Francis the place he loved
more than any other in the world, and the Portiuncula
would remain the center of the Franciscan order.
Now that the Catholic Church had accepted and
legitimatized Francis, all of Assisi embraced him as well.

He was asked to preach in the cathedral and some people actually bowed to him in the streets! Men came from all over Italy to join the Franciscan order, and in a few years they would come from all over the world.

The Lady Clare joins the Brothers

About a year after Francis and his followers took over the Portiuncula, a young woman from one of Assisi's most honored families ran away from home to join the Brothers Minor. The Lady Clare was tall and fair, with long golden hair. Her father owned a castle on the slope of Mount Subasio and a palazzo in the city. Clare was twelve when she first heard Francis preach in the streets of Assisi, and from that day on she silently admired him and prayed for him. Much of her time was spent in prayer and service to the poor, and she made a firm resolve that she would never marry, but would become the bride of Christ.

Somehow Clare communicated her need to Francis and he met with her. He knew intuitively that she belonged to God, and he agreed to accept her in the order. On the night of Palm Sunday, in the year 1212, when the Lady Clare was eighteen, she slipped out of her house and, accompanied by an aunt who was also a spiritual seeker, went through the forest to join the brothers.

As the ladies neared the Portiuncula, they were met by all the brothers, carrying torches and singing their welcome. Inside the sanctuary, Clare knelt before the altar and took her vows. Francis cut off her hair and gave her a cross-shaped tunic. Since there was no place for her to stay at Portiuncula, Francis took her to a convent not far away and asked the nuns to keep her until he could find a suitable place for her to stay.

On the following day Clare's family came looking for her with fire in their eyes. But when they found her and she bared her shorn head and told them of her love for

God, and her dedication to serving Him, they accepted her decision and went away peaceably.

A week later, however, Clare was joined by her fifteen-year-old sister Catherine; and now the enraged family mounted a twelve-man expedition to "rescue" both of the young women. When the horsemen approached the convent, the terrified nuns hid the sisters in the chapel, but the men stormed the doors and literally dragged Catherine out while Clare, in prayer before the altar, asked God to protect her little sister. According to the story, God answered Clare's prayer by making Catherine so heavy that her brothers could not carry her, and they finally gave up and left her on the ground, unhurt.

After Clare and her sister (whose name was changed to Agnes by Francis) lived for a while with the nuns, Francis received another welcome gift from the Benedictines—the church at St. Damian, whose chapel was the first he had repaired—and the second order of Franciscans, called the Poor Clares, was installed there. Like the Brothers Minor, the Sisters grew rapidly in numbers. The mother of Clare and Agnes joined them, as well as other women of the family. Over the years Clare became a powerful voice for the Franciscan Order, and even the Pope sought counsel from her.

But to Clare's disappointment the women were never allowed complete freedom to carry their message into the world. They remained cloistered. But, like the men, they nursed the lepers and fed the poor. They also sewed and spun and grew vegetables and flowers. And they had one important advantage—more time to spend in contemplation of God.

Like the brothers, the women tried always to keep the name of Jesus Christ on their lips. Throughout their waking hours, whether scrubbing, cooking, gardening, tending the sick or dying patients, or sitting in the chapel in meditation, they constantly repeated God's name, either

silently or softly. And God, who always responds to those
who call out His name, was with them constantly.

The third order–detachment while living in the world

In later years, a third order of Franciscans was
created. It came about in a natural way as a result of a
growing enthusiasm among the populace for giving up the
worldly life and joining Francis of Assisi. It so happened
that a wealthy landowner wanted to leave everything and
join the brothers, but Francis turned him down.

"Stay where you are," Francis said. "You can live
the life of Christ in the midst of your worldly duties. All
you need do is renounce sin, feed the poor, pray without
ceasing. Dedicate all your words, thoughts and deeds to
God, and He will reward you by giving you His constant
presence." Over succeeding years thousands of men and
women joined the Third Order. Their love and reverence
for the precepts of Christ, as demonstrated for them by the
life of Francis, helped to raise and reinforce the tottering
walls of Christianity.

To say that Francis had a way with animals is a
profound understatement. According to the stories handed
down, animals of all kinds were so drawn to Francis that
they behaved almost as though in ecstasy. Especially birds.
Once when Francis, exhausted, lay under a tree to rest,
hundreds of birds fluttered to him, beating their wings
rapidly and uttering cries of delight. Many landed on his
body and lowered their heads as though bowing to him.

We all have heard of how St. Francis preached a
sermon to the birds and literally thousands of birds came
to listen, gathering about him and bowing and chirping
their praise. On another occasion a fisherman presented
the saint with a fresh-caught fish. Francis thanked the
man, warned the fish not to allow itself to be caught again,
and put it back in the water. The fish showed its thanks by

performing an ecstatic wriggling dance for Francis before
sinking back into the depths.

The voracious wolf of Gubbio

But the most memorable animal story of all may be
the narrative of the wolf that terrorized the people of the
village of Gubbio. The wolf was huge, and it had killed
livestock and children alike. The wolf had lost all fear of
humans, and no one in the area was safe. The people of
Gubbio had built a high wall to protect themselves, and
they never unlocked the gate to go outside unless they
were well-armed with spears and pitchforks.

Answering the villagers' pleas for help, Francis
went to Gubbio to offer assistance. After listening to their
lurid tales of the vicious beast, he and one of his brothers
left the protection of the village walls and walked unarmed
into the forest to search for the wolf. Francis cautioned his
brother to stay well behind him as they followed a path
into the woods.

Shortly, Francis's companion was frozen with
horror as he saw the huge wolf burst out of the underbrush
and approach Francis at a run. Francis stood still, held up a
hand and spoke sharply to the wolf in the name of Christ.
Instantly the wolf stopped in its tracks and stood
there looking at Francis. Approaching the animal and
making the sign of the cross over its head, the saint told
the beast it must never again harm a human being. Francis
promised the wolf that it would be well fed, and that in
return it must agree to live peaceably with the citizens of
Gubbio. Francis's companion, astounded, watched as the
wolf bowed its head and wagged its tail and, to signify its
agreement with the conditions laid down by Francis,
extended its paw to shake the saint's hand.

Francis and the wolf walked back, side by side, to
the village, and Francis explained to the stunned citizens

that their own sins had brought about the predations of the wolf. If they would ask for forgiveness, accept God's help, and also promise to feed the wolf daily, there would be no more attacks.

The villagers repented, the bargain was struck, and the wolf actually became a kind of village mascot and even a household pet to the people of Gubbio. They allowed the wolf to go in and out of their homes, and the animal grew fat and lazy over the following years. The whole town mourned when the animal died, and it was given a Christian burial in a shrine dedicated to St. Francis of Assisi.

Could such a thing really happen? God only knows. But, actually, is such a story any more remarkable than the miracles that happen every day in the lives of men and women whose hearts have been touched by the Divine Beloved? If God can transform a human being, why not an animal? Furthermore, there is some evidence that the wolf story is more than a charming fairy tale. In 1873, when the ancient chapel in the town of Gubbio was being repaired and rebuilt, the skull of a large wolf was uncovered.

The crowning event in the life of Francis of Assisi was his attainment of union with his beloved Savior. It was the night of September 14, 1224, near the summit of LaVerna Mountain. Francis was forty-two years old at the time, and only about seventeen years had passed since he had totally abandoned the worldly life and begun to walk in the footsteps of Jesus.

Lights, fire and the stigmata

Francis was meditating on the suffering of Christ. His three companions slept some distance away. Brother Leo was awake, trying to keep an eye on Francis, who rested at the mouth of a cave beside a steep dropoff into the valley below.

Leo heard and saw marvelous and mysterious phenomena that night. He saw a seraph with wings of fire holding an image of the crucified Christ descend to anoint St. Francis. Reportedly people in villages nearby awoke and saw a tremendous light envelop the summit of LaVerna.

During the experience Francis received the stigmata—the wounds of the crucified Christ were imprinted on his body. Historians differ as to what this really means, but no less a spiritual authority than Avatar Meher Baba tells us that St. Francis became God-realized at that time. Since Francis had no living master to give him Realization, Baba said, God Himself sent his agent Khizr to earth to perform that function for his loving son Francis.

After that night on LaVerna Mountain, Francis had nothing to gain or to seek. The remainder of his short life was spent in saying his goodbyes to his dear brothers and sisters, his animal friends, and his beloved earth. The wounds of the stigmata bled almost constantly. Even though he wore long sleeves in an effort to conceal the wounds, people everywhere heard about it, and they came in droves to see Francis and to try to touch him.

As his death approached, his companions feared that the crowds might cut Francis's clothes to pieces for relics. In the minds of some of his followers, there was even the fear that, when the saint died, the relic-seeking masses might literally tear his body apart. Near the end Francis suffered constantly and was almost blind. (Some observers suggested that his visual difficulties were caused by the blinding light on the mountaintop. Others said: after seeing God, why would he want to observe the world around him?). In any case, for about two months Francis remained in total darkness in a room at San Damiano, where Clare and her nuns cared for him.

During his final illness he composed his poetic masterpiece, "The Canticle of the Sun." Francis wrote it

in a burst of inspiration, then called Sister Clare and his
brothers to listen as he sang it in a melody of his own
creation. He asked his companions to sing it every day,
and he himself sang it nearly every morning and evening,
despite long periods of intense suffering–suffering, we
should add, that was tempered by the infinite bliss and
peace which sustained him for the remainder of his days
on earth.

We conclude this account of Brother Francis with
his great poem, which remains a living testimonial to his
love for God and God's creation.

The Canticle of the Sun

– from *God's Fool, the Life and Times of Francis of Assisi,* by Julien Green and
translated by Peter Heinegg. Copyright © Editions du Seuil, Avril 1983. ©1985 by Harper
& Row, Publishers, Inc. Reprinted by permission of HarperCollins Publishers, Inc.

Most high, omnipotent, loving Lord,
To You alone belong praise and glory, honor and blessing.
No man is worthy to breathe Your name.

Be praised, my Lord, for all Your creatures.
In the first place for the blessed Brother Sun
Who gives us the day and enlightens us through You.

He is beautiful and radiant with his great splendor,
Giving witness of You, most Omnipotent One.

Be praised, my Lord, for Sister Moon and the stars
Formed by You so bright, precious, and beautiful.

Be praised, my Lord, for Brother Wind
And the airy skies, so cloudy and serene;
For every weather, be praised, for it is life-giving.

Be praised, my Lord, for Sister Water,
So necessary yet so humble, precious, and chaste.

Be praised, my Lord, for Brother Fire,
Who lights up the night,
He is beautiful and carefree, robust and fierce.

Be praised, my Lord, for our sister, Mother Earth,
Who nourishes and watches us
While bringing forth abundant fruits with colored flowers
And herbs.

Praise and bless the Lord.
Render Him thanks.
Serve Him with great humility. Amen

Milarepa: Great Yogi of Tibet
(1052 - 1136)

All worldly pursuits have one inevitable end,
which is sorrow. Acquisitions end in dispersion;
buildings, in destruction; meetings, in separations;
births, in deaths. Knowing this, one should
renounce acquisition and heaping up, and building,
and meeting; and, faithful to the commands
of a Master, set about to realize the Truth.

–Milarepa

Many centuries ago, in the ice-bound heights of the Himalayas, a hunter and his hound were pursuing a stag, which bounded up a steep slope and disappeared into a cave. The yelping dog followed, and the hunter, breathless from the chase, pulled himself up the rocky incline. Bow and arrow drawn, he ventured into the cave to confront his quarry.

To his astonishment, he saw that the cave was inhabited. A religious recluse–an anchorite–sat on a pallet wearing only a cotton loincloth. Lying on either side of the man were the stag and the hound. The animals gazed adoringly at the hermit as he sang to them in a sweet, melodious voice. The hermit was barely skin and bones, but his face radiated peace and good will. He sang about a stag and a hound and a hunter, and the evils of killing. "Conquer yourself, not others," he sang. "Detachment in this life leads to bliss in the next."

The words struck deep into the hunter's heart. He renounced the world and became a disciple of the hermit, who was Jetsun Milarepa, the great Tibetan yogi.

Stories of Milarepa's love for animals are reminiscent of tales of Saint Francis of Assisi, who a hundred years later would be preaching sermons to birds and reasoning with a wolf. Among the thousands of songs written by Milarepa are hymns to pigeons, tigers, elks and bears. Both Francis and Milarepa endured great hardships and displayed one-pointed perseverance and devotion in their quest for God.

Milarepa's path was perhaps even steeper than Francis's. Before Milarepa found a master who led him onto the spiritual path, he wielded the awesome power of black magic to destroy the crops of villagers who had been his neighbors. Even worse, he was guilty of the premeditated murder of dozens of people. Although Milarepa was a Buddhist (a follower of what has been described as a "Godless" path), it would be difficult to find a case that better illustrates the Christian concepts of sin, redemption and salvation, or which demonstrates more clearly that God's grace is not limited by religion, creed, time or place.

Jetsun Milarepa was born in August (on the twenty-fifth day of the lunar month) in the year 1052 in the village of Tsang-Tsa, near the present town of Kirong. The village was located about fifty miles north of the present city of Katmandu near the border of Nepal and Tibet. The community was built on the slopes of Mount Gosainthan, whose awesome height of 26,290 feet was overshadowed to the east by towering Mount Everest, a half-mile higher.

Jetsun was the only son and the first child of Mila-Sherab-Gyaltsen and his wife Karmo-Kyen ("White Garland"). Mila was the family surname, and for many generations only one male heir had been born. This boy-child was given the name Thopaga ("Delightful-to-Hear"). As he grew older, he proved to have a beautiful singing voice, and people said he was well-named. In later life he would be called Jetsun Milarepa, so we shall refer to him by that name.

His father, grandfather and great-grandfather were traders. In winter they traveled south to India to deal in wool, while in summer they bartered for cattle in the north. All were devout Buddhists, and his grandfather was known for his ability to "exorcise" or disperse hailstorms that threatened the barley fields on which the village depended. The family owned extensive farmland, and Jetsun grew up in a three-story house built on pillars. It was one of the finest structures in the area and was known as "The Four Columns and Eight Pillars."

When Jetsun was four, his sister Peta was born. Their mother, White Garland, was known for her beauty, and she came from the royal family of the Tsang province, where they lived. White Garland loved fine things, and she enjoyed plaiting the children's hair with pins of gold and turquoise.

When Jetsun was seven, his father was stricken by a devastating illness. He was treated by the best physicians in the region, and lamas also came to attend to his spiritual needs. But it was soon evident that Mila-Sherab would soon expire, and all the relatives and neighbors gathered in the room while the dying man dictated his last will and testament, which was signed, sealed and read aloud in the presence of all. Then he said:

"I know that my time is near, and my son, who will inherit my wealth, is still a child. Therefore, I entrust him to the care of all of you, my relatives, and especially my dear brother and his dear wife. All of my worldly goods and possessions, including my herds of cattle and sheep; my goats, ponies and donkeys; my fields and granaries; this house and all its furnishings; and also the care of my loving wife and infant daughter; all this I entrust to the care of all my relatives, but most especially to you two, my son's uncle and aunt."

He closed his eyes, breathed deeply several times

and continued. "When my son comes of age, and when his betrothed, Zesay [a maternal cousin], becomes his bride, the two of them will be given charge of all the property and they will follow in the footsteps of their parents. Until then, you, my brother, are responsible for my property and my family. See that they come to no harm, and be sure that I will be watching from the realm of the dead!" With that, his head fell forward and he died.

Deceived and robbed by relatives

As soon as the funeral was over, the aunt and uncle wasted no time in taking over everything—the land and animals, the silks, granaries, and utensils of gold, silver, copper, and iron, the ornaments and wardrobes. White Garland and her children were forced to labor in the barley fields in summer and to spin wool in winter. They were given scraps to eat and rags to wear. The children's long black hair, once braided and pinned with turquoise and gold, was now unkempt and infested by lice. The whole village talked about the cruel and inhuman treatment they were receiving.

Fortunately, they still had their home (even though most furnishings and jewelry had been removed), and White Garland still owned a small field that had been hers before marriage. When Jetsun reached the age of fifteen, his mother made plans to regain the estate. With the yield from the sale of barley from her field, she planned an elaborate feast. Sheep were butchered, brown barley was brewed into a beer called *chhang*, and white barley was ground into flour for baking bread and cakes. Carpets and draperies were borrowed from sympathetic friends and relatives. Curried mutton, rice, lentils and chutney were served, along with foaming mugs of chhang.

After the guests had eaten and drunk their fill, White Garland got her husband's will and read it aloud to the group. Then she said, "We are grateful to my dear husband's brother and his wife for taking care of our interests for all these years. But now Jetsun is old enough to manage the property and to marry Zesay, as my husband wished. So we respectfully request that all property be turned over to Jetsun as provided in Mila-Sherab's will."

She finished and sat down amid dead silence. Finally the aunt, pale with anger, rose and stamped her foot. "Everybody knows that Mila-Sherab-Gyaltsen did not own the property mentioned in that will." She curled her lip. "That will was a joke. We didn't have the heart to contradict a man whose brain was addled by his disease. So we humored him. The fool never owned a thing he didn't buy with money borrowed from us."

"That is a lie," said Jetsun's mother, flushing. "You are trying to rob my son of his inheritance."

The uncle stood up. "Everything my wife says is true. Everybody knows that my brother borrowed from us constantly. Even this house you are living in was built with my money."

White Garland stared, speechless, then looked helplessly about for support from her friends and relatives. But none came. Everybody was shocked with disbelief and afraid to confront Jetsun's uncle and his three husky sons, who now stood beside him.

The uncle shook his robes with disdain. "You ungrateful wretch! We have allowed you to live in this house out of pity for your children. But nothing we do for you is good enough. You get no more help from us." He and his wife stalked out, followed by their sons and other relatives who took their side. At the door, the uncle turned and sneered. "If you are strong enough, fight us. If you are not, cast spells on us."

"Oh, Mila-Sherab-Gyaltsen!" White Garland screamed. "You promised to watch over us from the realm of the dead. Have you forsaken us? How much more can we endure?" She collapsed and fell, sobbing, to the floor.

The remaining relatives stayed behind to offer their sympathies to White Garland, and to finish up the chhang. They all decided that the only course was to take up a collection to send Jetsun away to school, so that he might earn a living to support his mother and sister. In the meantime, his maternal uncle and Zesay's family would help White Garland by contributing flour, butter and fuel. Above all, they agreed, the widow and daughter of Mila-Sherab-Gyaltsen would not have to stoop to begging in the streets.

Jetsun began attending a small school for boys run by a popular teacher in a nearby village. The boy was quick and intelligent, and he enjoyed learning, so he was quite happy. Zesay often came to visit him, and they talked of someday getting married and having their own home and barley farm.

One day after school, Jetsun attended a dinner in honor of his teacher and drank freely of the abundant liquor. Walking home, he broke into song, exercising his strong, vibrant voice. His mother, who was roasting barley inside the house, could not believe her ears. Her son was singing merrily, oblivious of his family's humiliation and poverty.

Dropping her roasting tongs and leaving the barley to burn in the pan, she seized a handful of ashes and a rod and stormed out of the house. Throwing the ashes in her son's face and striking his head with the rod, she berated him soundly. Shrieking out her frustrations at the skies, she cried, "Oh, Mila-Sherb-Gyaltsen, look what a son you have left me with! Surely it cannot be your blood that flows in the veins of this vagabond. Oh, look what your family has come to!" She fell to the ground, sobbing.

Sobered by his mother's tears and the accusing eyes of his little sister, who stood watching, Jetsun begged forgiveness. "What would you have me do, Mother? I'll do anything you ask; anything to make you happy."

Her eyes narrowed. "I want you to study and learn the black arts. I want you to become a powerful sorcerer. I want you to take revenge on your aunt and uncle and their descendants to the ninth generation. Will you do that for your mother, son?"

He swallowed. "If that's what you really want, and we can somehow get the money. But, Mother, you are so full of hate. My teacher says good begets good and evils begets evil. If we use black magic, won't we accumulate a burden of evil that will bind us to the wheel of karma for many lifetimes?"

White Garland is bent on revenge

She tossed her head. "I don't believe that stuff. Power is what counts, son. A great sorcerer can control the weather and the lives of people. Who knows what happens in the realm of the dead? Your father said he would protect us, didn't he, and would punish those who harmed us?"

Jetsun nodded glumly.

"But he hasn't protected us. Why? Because he doesn't have the power. That's the only answer. The dead are dead, my son, but we're alive. It's up to *us* to punish our enemies. Do you recall the parting taunt of your uncle after he humiliated us before our guests?"

He nodded, tight-lipped. "Yes."

"He dared us to fight them if we were strong enough; and, if not, to cast spells on them. My son, let us act on his words. Through the black arts of sorcery, we will punish them all and cut off the root of their posterity."

"But how can I learn the black arts? We are poor."

"Give me your promise that you will do as I say, and I will find the money. I have heard of a great teacher of sorcery in the north country, and I will send you there."

So he promised, and she sold half of her plot of
land, for which she received a sky-blue turquoise gem, a
white pony, two loads of white sugar and two loads of
madder (*Rubia tinctorum*), a valuable herb whose roots are
used in dyeing cloth a brilliant red. The sugar was sold for
gold to meet Jetsun's traveling expenses and to pay his
tuition for a year of study. The pony was for him to ride
through the high mountains. He carried the turquoise stone
with him, and the madder was slung in bags across the
pony's back.

Seeking a guru of the black arts

His mother traveled with him for some distance,
constantly impressing on him the importance of his
mission. When they finally said their goodbyes, she held
him close and told him, through her sobs, that he must
succeed at all costs. "My son," she said, "never for a
moment allow yourself to forget what a wretched state we
have been reduced to—all because of your evil aunt and
uncle. I tell you truly, my son, that if you return home
without showing visibly the power to destroy our enemies,
I swear to you that I will kill myself in your presence."

He rode off sick with anguish at his mother's
parting words, and with the resolve to develop the occult
powers needed to carry out her will. Upon arrival at the
ashram of Lama Yungtun-Trogyal (Wrathful and
Victorious Teacher of Evil), Jetsun gave the sorcerer all
his gold and madder and the turquoise gem, asking only
that in return he be fed and clothed for as long as it took
him to learn how to wreak havoc on those who had robbed
him of his inheritance.

After a year of study the guru presented each of his
students with a fine woolen coat and bade them farewell.
The others departed, but Jetsun Milarepa was not at all
satisfied. He felt he had not learned enough to produce

any real effect on his enemies; and he was consumed with fear that his mother would, as she had threatened, actually kill herself in his presence if he failed.

So he called on his guru and begged for further teachings, telling him in graphic detail what had happened to his mother and little sister and himself after his father died. The guru was reduced to tears by the story, and he told Milarepa he would make inquiries. If the story was confirmed, he would teach him "the real Art."

The guru had a disciple who, through his occult power, was faster than a horse and stronger than an elephant. This disciple was dispatched to Tsang-Tsa to investigate; and when he returned a few days later he told the teacher that everything the young man had told him was true. So the guru said to Jetsun. "I withheld the real Art from you for fear you would misuse the power. But now that I know you are truthful, and you have been severely wronged, I will give you the whole Art. I can teach you to launch hail-storms and guide them with the tips of your fingers; but I will first send you to a colleague who will teach you to kill at long distance."

The second sorcerer directed him to build a model structure along the lines of his uncle's house at Tsang-Tsa and to remain in the structure for seven days chanting a special incantation which included the names of the thirty-five persons he wished to kill. Just to be sure, Jetsun continued the chanting for fourteen days. During the last day, the teacher showed him in a vision the bleeding heads and hearts of thirty-five persons. "But I note," the teacher said, "that there are two other persons who should be sacrificed." He was referring to the hated aunt and uncle, who were not included in the thirty-five deaths.

"No," Jetsun said. "My mother wants them to be spared so she can gloat over them. She says that killing is too good for them."

The guru shook his head. "I wouldn't want to have

your mother on my case."

That night, in the village of Tsang-Tsa, the oldest son of Jetsun Milarepa's uncle was being married, and all those who had sided with the aunt and uncle were invited to the wedding feast. Their house, like many higher class Tibetan homes, was raised on pilings, with the ground level used as a stable for horses.

Murder through sorcery

At the same time in the sorcerer's ashram, Jetsun was chanting his incantation of death, calling up a horde of evil astral entities. In Tsang-Tsa one of the uncle's servants went outside to fetch water. He was terrified to see monstrous snakes and toads digging at the base of the house. Clawing at the main support was a scorpion the size of a yak. The servant shrieked in horror and the horses, which were tied to the pillars, stampeded, shaking the foundation so hard that the house collapsed, killing the thirty-five people condemned by Jetsun. The aunt and uncle escaped with minor injuries.

Before the dust had settled and the bodies had been removed, White Garland, unable to contain her cruel joy, marched up and down the street, waving a flag and boasting of her son's powers of sorcery. Shocked by her vindictiveness, many of her neighbors who had earlier sympathized with her now turned against her. Her brother-in-law, mad with grief over the loss of all his sons, came to strangle her, but was restrained by a neighbor who suggested it would be far better to kill the son first, and then the mother, to prevent retaliation. Passions in the village became so inflamed that a band of armed men was formed to search the surrounding hills for Jetsun. There was talk of using force to induce White Garland to reveal the whereabouts of her son.

White Garland sold the remaining half of her land

for seven pieces of gold. She wanted to send the gold to Milarepa, along with a personal message, but she didn't know whom she could trust. Then, as luck would have it, a pilgrim from the north who was returning home from a visit to sacred shrines in Nepal came to her door begging alms. She learned that he was acquainted with the area where Jetsun was staying, so she showered him with hospitality, allowing him to stay in her home for several days and feeding him well.

She prayed to her favorite deities and felt she had received their assurance that the pilgrim was trustworthy. So she offered to pay him well to deliver a sealed letter to her son who, she assured him, would also pay him a like sum upon delivery. In the meantime, while mending the pilgrim's cloak-blanket, she sewed a large black patch on the cloak and covered it with seven stars, representing the constellation known as the Pleiades. Under each of the stars she hid a piece of gold.

In her letter to Jetsun she congratulated him for his impressive display of sorcery and warned him that the villagers now felt hatred for him and his family and were conspiring against them. She urged him to launch a violent hail-storm to convince the people to leave them alone. She also told him that if he needed money he should search for a valley facing north, overshadowed by a dark cloud and lit by the seven stars known as the Pleiades. There, she added, he would find seven of their relatives who would help him.

After the pilgrim reached the area where Milarepa was staying, he found him and gave him the letter. Unable to make sense of the reference to seven stars, Milarepa asked the pilgrim to wait while he showed the letter to his guru, who read the letter and said: "You have a very vindictive mother. Many people have already been killed and she orders you to launch a hail-storm! Will she ever have enough blood on her hands? But what is this about your relatives?"

"I don't know, master. We have no relatives in the north that I know of."

But the guru's wife was keenly intelligent, and after reading the letter asked to see the pilgrim, whom she invited to join them for a feast. A big fire was built and much chhang was served, and soon the pilgrim removed his cloak. The guru's wife playfully put the cloak on her own back and danced around, saying, "Happy are they who wear the same cloak no matter where they go." After a while she left the room, still wearing the cloak, and went up on the roof-terrace, where she examined it carefully, found and removed the gold pieces and then sewed the patches back in place. She gave the cloak back to the pilgrim, served him dinner, and showed him a room where he could spend the night.

Jetsun was astonished when his guru's wife gave him seven pieces of gold and explained how she had solved the riddle of the seven stars. After rewarding the pilgrim and giving part of the gold to his guru, he returned to his first teacher to learn the incantations and invocations required to generate and direct hail-storms.

When his teacher told him he was ready, he went overland, along with the man who was swift as a horse and strong as an elephant, to his old village of Tsang-Tsa. Disguised as pilgrims, they walked about freely and could see that the barley fields were ripe with grain ready for picking. The harvest that year was so abundant that the authorities had decreed that no one would be allowed to harvest any crops until a date selected when all harvesting would begin at once. This was done to prevent unfair competition by rushing one's grain to market ahead of the other growers. The big harvest was scheduled to begin in a few days.

From a bluff overlooking the fields, Milarepa began chanting his special hail-storm mantra. Soon a huge

black cloud formed and settled over the valley. A violent
hail-storm burst from the cloud, battering the fields,
carving deep gorges and pulverizing every ear of grain in
the fields. When the storm lifted, a great wail of distress
welled up from the throats of all the villagers who had lost
the crops they had labored long and hard to produce.

Tortured by remorse, he craves forgiveness

The cries were like a blow to Jetsun's heart, and he
found himself weeping uncontrollably. While escaping and
returning to the black magician's ashram, he and his
companion had several narrow escapes and Jetsun was
bitten by a dog.

Milarepa was now tortured by remorse for his
black deeds. He longed so fervently for divine forgiveness
that he hardly ate or slept. He yearned to find a master
who could lead him toward the light, but he could not
bring himself to discussing the matter with his guru of the
black arts.

Finally, one day, when a wealthy supporter of the
guru fell ill and died, the guru said to Jetsun Milarepa,
"Last night, when my excellent patron passed away, it was
as if I felt a knife in my cold heart. All my life, from my
days as a youth, I have spent my time causing pain and
death to others through use of the black arts." He sighed
and laid his hand on Jetsun's head. "And you, too, my son,
have taken the same sinful path. You have already earned
for yourself a pile of evil karma, like a stinking heap of
manure; and your karma, my son, increases my load as
well since I am responsible for your evil acts."

"I begged you to teach me, Sir. I can't blame you."

The guru shook his head. "I am to blame—for you
and for countless others who have taken this path." He
paused. "But it is not too late. Are you ready to change
your life and take the Path of Light, the path of love and

emancipation, my son?"

Tears welled up in Jetsun's eyes and he nodded. "There is nothing I want more."

The guru smiled. "Good! So here is what I propose. If you wish to remain here as guardian for my children and disciples, I will go and work for my own salvation, and also for yours. Or, if you prefer, *you* can go and learn the Holy Dharma on my behalf as well as on your own, and I will provide you with all necessary material support."

In quest of a true master

Jetsun was overjoyed by his good fortune. His guru provided him with a yak and a load of fine woolen cloth and directed him to go to a famous lama at a place called Nar. The lama received him, initiated him and gave him instructions. A few days later, however, the lama told him that he couldn't help him. "As you told me, you are a great sinner, and I fear your sins are too great for me to eradicate. However, a great teacher named Marpa the Translator lives at a place called Wheat Valley. There is a karmic link from past lives connecting you to this great yogi Marpa, so you must go to him."

The instant Milarepa heard the name "Marpa the Translator," he felt a great thrill pass through his body. Every hair seemed to be waving in ecstasy, and tears of joy flowed from his eyes. With great excitement he set out to find his master.

When he drew near Wheat Valley, he began questioning people about where the great yogi, Marpa the Translator, lived. No one seemed to know. A woman carrying a pitcher of milk on her head told him that a man named Marpa lived nearby, but she didn't know anything about a yogi or a translator. Milarepa asked her the name of the area they were in, and she said it was known as the

Ridge of the Dharma. Encouraged, he kept going.

Soon after, he asked a group of cowherders if they knew where he could find the yogi known as Marpa the Translator, and one young man said, "You must mean my father. His name is Marpa. He used to sell off everything in our house and go to India and then come back with many rolls of paper. If he's the one you're looking for, he's right around the bend plowing a field."

Jetsun thanked him and continued on his way. He very much doubted that a great spiritual teacher would be out plowing a field; but when he saw a heavyset lama plowing a field, he suddenly had a feeling of such joy and inexpressible bliss that he briefly lost consciousness of his surroundings.

Recovering, he approached the man and said, "Reverend Sir, can you tell me where I can find the great yogi, Marpa the Translator?"

The lama looked him up and down and replied, "Where do you come from, and why are you here?"

"I'm a great sinner from the highlands of Tsang. My soul needs deliverance from my many black deeds. I want to find salvation for my sick soul."

The lama nodded and wiped his brow. Removing his hat, he took from it a clay flask of chhang, which he handed to the youth. "Have a drink," he said. "If you'll finish my plowing for me, I'll go up to the house and see if I can arrange an appointment with him. Keep plowing this field until someone comes to get you. And see that you do a good job." He walked up the hill toward a large house.

Jetsun finished the beer and started plowing. The day was warm and he worked up quite a sweat before the young cowherder he had spoken to earlier came down the hill and asked him to follow him to where he would meet Marpa.

"First, let me finish plowing this field," said Jetsun.

"Since that kind lama managed me get me an introduction with the famous Marpa the Translator, the least I can do is finish plowing his field for him." So he completed the plowing and then followed the young man to a room where the lama sat on two cushions. Jetsun was quite sure the seated man was the same one who had been plowing the field, so he looked around to see if another lama was in the room.

The seated man said, "Of course you didn't recognize me, but I am Marpa."

Bowing to the lama and touching his feet with his forehead, Jetsun said, "Beloved Master, I am a great sinner from the highlands. I have come to offer my body, mind and soul to you. I pray you will provide me with food, clothing and spiritual instruction and enable me to attain Liberation in this lifetime."

"What sins have you committed?" the lama asked. After listening carefully to Jetsun Milarepa's account of his loss of birthright and his use of sorcery to kill and to destroy, he said, "I will give you spiritual instruction, but you will have to provide your own food and clothing. Whether or not you can attain Liberation in one lifetime depends entirely on your energy and perseverance and how hard you are willing to work."

Jetsun nodded. "I have come to you for the Truth, Master. I will work hard and I will obey, and I will find my food and clothes elsewhere." So for weeks he went begging up and down the fertile valley, obtaining bags of barley, some of which he bartered for meat, chhang and a heavy copper pot. Proud of his efforts and exhausted by the exertion, he carried everything into the lama's house and dropped it on the floor with a loud clatter.

"Are you trying to shake the house down?" shouted his guru. "Put those filthy sacks outside!"

Later Marpa accepted the offerings, but seemed to do so in a grudging manner. Jetsun bowed to him and asked if he could now have spiritual instruction. Marpa replied: "First I have a job for you. In the highland provinces are many of my disciples and lay-followers who would like to come here and bestow presents upon me. However, those who have tried to come have been robbed by the nomad settlers of Yamdak and Talung. I want you to launch hail-storms on those districts to teach those robbers a lesson."

Jetsun was aghast. "You want me to use sorcery again to destroy property and perhaps kill people?"

"Yes. This is a religious duty I am assigning you. Later I will give you spiritual instructions on the path of Truth."

Jetsun bowed and went away. After launching massive hail-storms on the districts, he returned to Marpa and asked if he could now have the promised instructions.

"Are you serious!" demanded Marpa. "Do you really think that launching a few hail-storms should entitle you to the sacred Dharma, which I obtained through great cost and self-sacrifice from my revered guru Naropa in India? Now, if you are really sincere about seeking Truth, you will use your sorcery to destroy a band of Lhobrak hill-men, who have often robbed disciples of mine coming from Nyal-Lo-ro. If you will do that, I will impart to you the mystic truths by which one can achieve Liberation and attain Buddhahood in a single lifetime."

Again Jetsun did his master's bidding, putting a curse on the Lhobrak hill-people that caused a feud to break out among them, in the course of which many of them were killed or maimed. The fighting and bloodshed he had caused and observed gave Jetsun great remorse and anguish, and he prayed he would never have to use sorcery again. After he returned to his guru and told what had happened, Marpa told him he was indeed an adept at sorcery.

Standing before his master with his head bent in shame, he said, "May I now have the teachings, Sir?"

Marpa shook his head. "Do you really think you are entitled to the Holy Dharma, the most precious teachings that exist, in return for your having committed vile and evil deeds? What kind of exchange is that? Now, if you will go and compensate the hillfolk for all the destruction you caused; if you will restore to life those who were killed; then you will certainly be entitled to the truths you seek. If you cannot, then stay away from me."

Of course, Jetsun was plunged into black despair, and he wept bitterly, while Marpa's wife, who had never seen her husband treat an aspirant so cruelly, tried to comfort the young man.

Next day Marpa came to Jetsun and said, "I may have been a little hard on you yesterday, Great Sorcerer. Just be patient, and the time will come when you will have the teachings. In the meantime, you seem to be quite a versatile young man, and I wonder if you could build a house for one of my sons. If you do a good job, I'll give you the mystic truths. Also, I'll feed and clothe you while you are here."

"But Master," Milarepa said, "what if I happen to die before the dark stains of my sins have been wiped from my soul?"

"Don't worry about that. I promise that you will not die before you have been relieved of your evil karma. You have my assurance of that."

Building a stone house for Marpa

Jetsun sighed. "In that case, Master, I'll be happy to construct a house for your son. Have you drawn up any plans?"

Marpa took him to the top of a mountain ridge and pointed out a place where he would like to have built a circular house of stone. He told him he could obtain the stones and clay from a riverbed in the valley.

For months Jetsun Milarepa hauled stones which he sized and fitted neatly in position in a circle. When the structure was about half complete, Marpa showed up one day with a frown on his face. "I am afraid I didn't consider these plans as fully as I should have." He shook his head. "It won't do, Great Sorcerer. It just won't do."

"You mean you don't want me to finish it?"

"No. You'll have to tear it down. Take all the stones back to the riverbed and restore this spot as closely as possible to its original condition. After you've finished, I'll come up and inspect. By then, I'll have completed the new plans for the house."

After the backbreaking task of replacing all the building materials and cleaning up the grounds had been accomplished, Marpa took Jetsun to a new site and directed him to build a crescent-shaped house. When it was about half-completed, the guru came up and said that the location was not suitable. "Great Sorcerer, you will just have to tear it down and take the materials back where you got them." Again, without complaint, Jetsun obeyed.

Next, the lama took him to a different ridge and said apologetically, "Great Sorcerer, I must have been tipsy when I asked you to build that crescent-shaped house. It was a bad mistake. But now I know what I want, and you can build me a fine house on this spot." Jetsun said respectfully that it was an expensive proposition for Marpa, and a lot of trouble for Jetsun, to continue to build houses and then tear them down. He asked the lama to consider carefully before starting another project.

Marpa nodded. "Well put. But I'm not tipsy today, and I have indeed given the matter a great deal of thought. A mystic's dwelling should be triangular, so build me one of that shape. Don't worry. This one will not be torn down."

So Jetsun set to work with renewed vigor. When he had finished about a third of the structure, the lama

arrived and said, "What in the world are you doing? Who
told you to build a three-sided dwelling?"

"Why, you did. It's the house you said you wanted
for your son, Your Reverence, and you ordered me to build
it exactly like this."

"I don't remember ordering such a monstrosity. If
I told you to build a house like this, I was out of my mind."

"But, Your Reverence, I asked you to consider carefully, and you said you *had*, and that this house would not
be demolished. And if I may say so, Sir, you seemed to be
normal and to know exactly what you were doing."

The lama stared at him coldly. "Do you have a
witness for what you claim? Are you trying to destroy my
family and me by sorcery? The idea of putting anybody
into a triangular building! It looks like a magic triangle to
me. Young man, *I* am not the one who robbed you of your
inheritance. Don't take your spite out on me."

"But, Master," Jetsun said. "I swear to you—"

"Enough of swearing, and charms, and sorcery!
Tear down that ugly structure immediately and take all the
rocks and clay and tools back where you got them. When
you finish, I'll either send you away or give you some
spiritual instruction."

By then, Jetsun had a large sore on his back from
hauling heavy rocks. But he was afraid to mention it to
either the lama or the lama's wife. He did beg the wife,
however, to urge her husband to give him the promised
instruction, which she did. "Please take pity on that young
man," she said. "You are killing him. He is doing the best
he can." The lama asked her to prepare a nice dinner and
ask Jetsun to join them.

After they had eaten, the lama took the youth aside
and said, "Great Sorcerer, do not ever again falsely accuse
me of mistreating you. Now, here are the instructions I
promised you." He recited to him the Rules of Right
Conduct from the Buddhist Scriptures and other parts of

what is known as the Refuges. Then he added, "These are known as temporal religious instructions. If you want to go beyond these and obtain the mystic truths, you must first convince me that you deserve them." He paused and shook his head sadly. "I personally fear you may never be ready for *those* teachings."

Inwardly Jetsun Milarepa said to himself: I *will* be deserving. I *will* attain the highest teachings, and I *will* do everything my guru commands me to do.

Ordered to build a nine-story house

Later the lama invited him to go for a walk, taking him to a place where, Jetsun had been told, title to the land was in dispute and the contenders had all agreed not to build on the land. Marpa said, "I want you to build here a rectangular nine-story house, with an ornamental roof serving as the tenth story. This house will not be torn down. When it is completed, I will initiate you on the Path of Truth, and will feed and clothe you while you are per- forming the *sadhana* of meditation that I will prescribe for you."

"Reverend Sir," Jetsun ventured, "would you allow me to ask your wife, the Reverend Mother, to come and be witness to your wishes on this house?"

Marpa nodded. "Certainly. While you are going to get her, I'll just mark off the boundaries of the house on the ground."

After Marpa's wife had accompanied him to the spot, Jetsun said: "Reverend Sir and Reverend Mother. I have built and demolished three houses on the orders of my master. When I reminded him of what he had told me previously, he demanded to know who I could produce as a witness to his orders. Now he is asking me to build a nine-story house, so I beg of you, Reverend Mother, to be a witness to his orders."

"I'll gladly be a witness," she said, "but your guru is so headstrong he will pay absolutely no attention to us and what we say. Furthermore, the Reverend Father is ordering you to do something that is unneeded and useless. In addition, this plot of land is not legally ours, and the owners, your Guru's relatives, have stipulated that no building on this land will be allowed. However, I know that what I say will make no difference."

Marpa said, "Kindly do what is requested of you–namely act as witness–then go back home and leave me to handle my part of the business." Which she did without another word.

So Jetsun set about constructing the nine-story house. In jest, three leading disciples of the guru carried a huge boulder to the site and left it there, saying, "Here, Great Sorcerer, put this in your building." The boulder had a very nice shape, so Jetsun used it as a cornerstone, and he then proceeded to complete the first and second floors before the guru came to inspect. Walking about the structure, Marpa pointed to the large cornerstone and said, "Great Sorcerer, where did you get that stone?"

"Oh, it was brought here in jest by your chief disciples, Master."

"Is that a fact? Well, you were ordered to do all work on this house without help. Kindly remove that stone and take it back to where it came from."

"Reverend Father, you promised not to order me to tear this building down."

"I never gave you permission to use the labor of my chief disciples in constructing the building. Remove and return that stone and then continue with your work."

In order to remove the huge stone, Jetsun had to tear down parts of the first and second stories. After he had done that and rolled the stone laboriously back to where it had come from, his guru visited the site and nodded his approval, then said, "Now you can go back and get that big stone; bring it back here by your own efforts and put it back in the same place where it was." Which he accomplished during several days of superhuman effort, singlehandedly doing what three men had earlier done with considerable effort.

By the time four stories of the house had been erected, some of the owners of the land said, "It looks like Marpa really intends to have Great Sorcerer complete a house this time. Shouldn't we stop this foolishness before it goes any farther?"

But others said, "Let the lama have his fun. Before the house is half built, he'll order that young fool to tear it down again, just as he has done several times before."

Pressures mount, and a crisis approaches

However, by the time the seventh floor had been built, the landowners were getting more and more worried. They held a meeting and voted to go to the spot in a group and demolish the building. But when they got there they found a large force of armed troops stationed inside and around the structure. Marpa had used his higher occult powers to create the troops. His relatives were so awed and frightened that, en masse, they went to Marpa and bowed and paid their respects. Eventually they all became his disciples.

Soon after, an initiation ceremony for discipleship was held. Jetsun felt that surely Marpa would accept him now, so he took his seat with the other candidates. The lama, seeing him sitting there, said, "Great Sorcerer, what are you offering in return for initiation?"

"Your Reverence promised me initiation when I had completed the house for your son. Since the house is almost complete, I thought—"

"Well, you thought wrong!" shouted the lama. "Just because you've stacked up a few stones and slapped

some mud and clay down, you think I should impart to
you the sacred lore I obtained in India at great sacrifice
and expense! If you can pay the initiation fees, fine and
good. Show me the gold. If not, get your carcass out of
my mystic circle!" Grabbing the youth by his long hair, he
dragged him out of the room.

Milarepa wept all night, wishing he were dead.
Next day the lama's wife came and tried to console him.
"I don't know what's come over the master," she said.
"Ordinarily, his teachings are available to all beings who
cross his path. Even a vicious dog will be petted, fed and
prayed for. But don't lose heart, my son. Keep your faith
in your guru and you will eventually prevail."

To the brink of suicide and back—finally, acceptance
And so it turned out to be. Although Jetsun was
driven to the brink of suicide time after time, and he ran
away more than once, seeking another guru, he always
came back. And as his sufferings increased, he began to
realize that his treatment at the hands of a Realized Master
was a blessing in itself. Marpa knew from the start, of
course, that Jetsun Milarepa would become a great saint.
Each time he threatened, scolded, abased, demeaned or
thrashed the youth, he was ridding him of evil impressions
accumulated from his past.

And finally, of course, when his disciple's heart
had been purified by pain and despair, and his pride
reduced to humility, he was accepted. Marpa lovingly cut
Milarepa's hair, fed him by hand, and gave him the robe of
a priest.

Marpa gave him special instructions on meditation
and furnished him with ample provisions, and Milarepa
retired in seclusion to a tiny cave, where he saw not
another soul for eleven months. Finally Marpa and his
wife came to invite him to join them for a religious feast.

After spending a few relaxed days with them, he went back to his cave, freshly stocked with provisions, where he walled himself in and remained, with very little contact with the outside world, for many years. During this period, songs began to flow spontaneously from Milarepa's lips, a phenomenon that continued throughout his life.

One morning he awoke with his pillow wet with tears. He had dreamed that his family's home, Four Columns and Eight Pillars, was in ruins, his mother was dead and his sister was homeless and wandering about the countryside. He rose at dawn, tore down the wall at the entrance to his cave, and went to see his guru to beg permission to return to Tsang-Tsa for a visit.

"You may go if you wish," said Marpa, "but if you go, you are destined to never return to Wheat Valley." Tears filled the guru's eyes. "You and I, my son, will never meet again in this life. You will become a shining light for Buddhism, but you must always remember that your path to Liberation requires total renunciation."

Sad homecoming

Milarepa made the long trip home. On a hillside above the village, he could see his family home. He approached some shepherds and asked, "Can you tell me who lives in that large house?" They told him the story of the tragedy he knew so well; of how the son, after losing his inheritance, wreaked havoc on the village through black magic; how the mother had finally died and the daughter had wandered away somewhere, begging.

"Who lives there now?" asked Milarepa.

"Only ghosts and the bones of the mother, who died about eight years ago. No one will go inside the house for fear of the son's black magic."

Milarepa secluded himself until nightfall, then went into the village and entered the shell of his old home,

where he slept on the decaying floor. At dawn he saw that
the house was in ruins, as he had seen it in his dream. The
roof had collapsed, birds and mice were nesting in the
nooks and crannies, and a set of valuable sacred books had
been badly damaged by the elements. He found a heap of
cloth and earth containing human bones which he intuitively knew were the remains of his mother. Making a
pillow of the bones, he meditated on life and death and
came to the realization that, through his prayers, he could
relieve his mother and father of much of the suffering and
pain their disembodied or reincarnated souls were experiencing. He sank into a deep state of *samadhi,* where he
remained for seven days.

Awakening, he decided to dispose of his mother's
bones in the approved Buddhist manner–that is, to have
them ground them up and mixed with clay, and molded
into tiny memorial shrines, like miniature *stupas.* He
would offer the sacred books as payment to some
professional to perform the work. Then he would retire to
a secluded cave and sit in meditation day and night until
death overtook him.

He took the books to the house of a kindly teacher
who had taught him as a child. The teacher had died, and
his son was fearful of accepting the books because of
Milarepa's repution for sorcery. However, when assured
that no harm would befall him, he agreed to accept them
and to cast the bones into little stupas. After the work was
finished, and sacred rites were performed over the relics,
the teacher's son asked Milarepa to stay in his house for a
few days and tell him how he had become transformed
from a sorcerer into a religious devotee.

Milarepa told of his years of struggle and his
acceptance by the great guru Marpa. The teacher's son
nodded and said, "You will be a saint someday. However,
your guru is a householder with a wife and family, so why
can't you do the same? Your betrothed Zesay is a very

lovely woman, and she has waited all these years for you
to come home and marry her. Why don't you settle down,
marry Zesay, and fix up your house? You can live in
comfort and still maintain your inner life of prayer."

With tears flowing from his eyes, Milarepa
explained through a beautiful song that each person has
his own karma, and his own black deeds of his youth
could only be erased by a life of complete detachment as a
solitary hermit, and his guru had directed him to live in
that manner.

His teacher's son gave him butter, cheese, flour,
salt and water, wished him luck and asked for his prayers.
Milarepa climbed up to a cave in a bluff above his house
and sat in meditation. Using his food only sparingly he
remained in the cave, without contact with the outside
world, for several months. Finally, gaunt and weak from
hunger and his provisions exhausted, he went to beg from
herdsmen camped in the valley.

His aunt sets her dogs on him

Approaching a yak-hair tent, he called out, begging
for alms of bread and butter and cheese. To his dismay,
an enraged, screaming woman whom he recognized as his
aunt set her dogs on him and flailed him with a tent pole.
Exhausted and bleeding, he fell to the ground and sang a
song of supplication, which moved his aunt to tears. She
gave him food and comfort, but his uncle, upon seeing
him, chased him away with stones and arrows and incited
young boys in the village to attack him with rocks and
sticks.

Milarepa decided he must move to a remote region
to escape the wrath of the villagers. But that night he was
told in a dream that he should stay a few days longer. He
did, and was surprised to see Zesay, his betrothed, who
brought him food and drink and embraced him lovingly.

She told him in detail the story of his mother's death, and how his sister had become a beggar.

"But you, Zesay, why have you never married?"

"Everybody was so afraid of your sorcery that no man would ask for my hand. They all knew I had been promised to you." She looked away. "And even if they had asked, I would have refused." She paused and bit her lip. "Understand, my friend. I consider it commendable of you to follow a religious life, but what are you going to do with your house and land?"

Milarepa closed his eyes and sighed. "If my sister returns, she should have the property. Until that happens, it is yours, Zesay. You may use the land for growing crops, or you can lease it out and keep the money."

"Don't you want to keep the field for the food it will produce?"

"No. I'll find my food as the birds and rodents find theirs. I prefer to live in the solitude of caves, so I have no use for a house or land. Even if I owned the whole world, I would have to give it up at death. By giving everything up now, I can achieve happiness in both this world and the next. There is much to be said for the religious life, Zesay. I think you should consider entering into it. But if not, the house and field are yours."

She shook her head. "I cannot take your house and land; they should go to your sister. I *would* like to be a religious devotee, but I cannot follow *your* path."

He held her hand. "I will probably not see you again, Zesay. I am crossing the mountain to the big white rock cave, where I will remain in meditation until death takes me. If you see my sister, tell her I send love." She nodded tearfully, kissed him and departed.

Soon after Zesay's visit, his aunt appeared with sacks of provisions. "You must leave, nephew," she said. "My neighbors live in terror that you will kill or harm us through sorcery. Take these goods in payment for your barley field, which you have no use for, anyway."

He accepted the sacks of food and clothing she brought and sang a heart-warming song of farewell. Embracing him, his aunt said, "The more I see of you, my nephew, the more impressed I am by your religious zeal. I'm beginning to understand why only a chosen few are able to climb the mountain of Illumination."

Over the next few days he moved his provisions to a larger and more remote cave in the white rock mountain, where he set up his abode with bedding and a meditation cushion. He vowed never to seek help from any village– not for food, clothing, medicine or any other necessities of life.

At this point he was discouraged with his lack of spiritual progress. For years he had been attempting to generate the vital warmth that allows advanced yogis to sit naked on the high peaks and, through internal heat alone, melt the ice and snow around them. However, due to his physical weakness from lack of nutritious food, he could not properly harness the inner fire and was still sensitive to the cold.

Success in generating the vital heat

He prayed to his guru for guidance. Soon after, he experienced a vision in which a group of women carrying various foods came and fed him and performed a *puja* in the name of his revered Marpa. Following instructions given by the women, he soon was able to generate the ecstatic warmth, and he thanked his guru inwardly for his guidance. After that, for about a year he spent most of his time, day and night, in samadhi.

One day he stood up and looked outside. The sky and trees were exceedingly beautiful, and he felt an urge to take a long walk and look at the glories of the natural world. But then he remembered his vows, so he sang a song of reproof to himself and sat back down to resume his meditation.

Three more years went by. His sack of barley flour was almost empty. He had allowed himself only twenty measures of flour a year, and now that was virtually gone. He considered the vows he had made and concluded that if he sought food without descending to a place inhabited by other humans, he would not be breaking his vows. So he walked outside the cave. Not far away, he found a sunny glen, with a rippling spring, a profusion of nettles and a good view of the snow-capped mountains.

For the next year he lived on nettle soup. His clothes had now worn out and his body was reduced to skin and bones. All day long, and often for many days without a break, he sat in the cross-legged lotus position. His skin, as green as the nettles, was covered by fine, greenish hair.

One day as he sat in the sunny glen in meditation, a group of hunters happened upon him. Startled by his appearance and thinking he was an evil spirit, they were about to run away, but he assured them he was a human being and quite harmless. Having had no luck finding game, they were hungry, and they searched his cave, then demanded to know where he kept his provisions.

"I have only nettles," he told them. "Even if I had other provisions, you would not get them by using force. That is not the way to accomplish one's aim in life."

"Oh, is that so?" said a burly man. Showing off for his companions, he lifted the cross-legged Milarepa up and let him fall to the ground. Laughing, two of the other men also lifted him up and dropped him, which was a very painful procedure for the bone-thin yogi. Despite his pain, Milarepa made no response except to shed sincere tears of sympathy for the ignorant men who had no idea of the karmic implications of their cruel acts.

One of the hunters interceded and tried to protect Milarepa. "This man may well be a holy lama or a true yogi," he said. "Even if he is not, you will not gain merit by mistreating such a weak, defenseless person." To Milarepa, he said, "I admire you for putting up with such treatment without complaint. I did not hurt you, my dear fellow, so please remember me in your prayers."

Milarepa smiled. "I will remember you, friend."

"Remember me, too," the burly man said, with a laugh. "I'm the one who lifted you up the highest."

"He'll remember *you*, all right," said the kinder man, "but not in the way you think."

Hunters reap karmic results of their cruelty

By this time, Milarepa had reached a high state of detachment, and he felt no anger, only pity, at the men's crude and cruel behavior. However, it appeared that karma (or divine retribution, if you choose) overtook the hunters rapidly. Not long after the visit, the hunters were arrested on an unrelated charge. The burly man was executed, and two others had their eyes put out. The only one to escape punishment was the man who had been kind to Milarepa. [This incident reminds us of a warning by Meher Baba that one should always be respectful to any God-absorbed or God-intoxicated soul. Mistreating an advanced soul can lead to devastating results.]

Months later another group of hunters carrying deer and other game they had killed approached the cave. Like the earlier group, they were startled and frightened by Milarepa's appearance. But when they realized he was a yogi, they showed respect and kindness to him, showering gifts of meat and other provisions on him. So, for weeks, he ate well and felt such happiness as he had never known.

One night he awoke to find a man stealthily searching his cave. Milarepa laughed aloud and said, "If you can find something at night that I could never find in the daytime, you are welcome to it!" The would-be burglar also laughed and went away.

About a year later some hunters from Milarepa's own village came. Finding the hermit in samadhi, they were unsure if he was alive or dead, so they prodded him with their spears. He awoke and they realized he must be Jetsun Milarepa. "We heard that you came back to your home on a visit, but that was many years ago. Have you been here all this time?"

He smiled. "I've been right here."

"We're hungry," one of them said. "Do you have any provisions?"

He offered to share his nettle soup with them; but with no salt or spices to flavor it, they could not tolerate the bitter soup. Spitting it out, one said, "If you're living on that stuff, you must be the most miserable creature in the world."

Milarepa smiled. "I am one of the happiest and most fortunate men in the world. Because of the grace of my revered guru Marpa, I have learned the path to Freedom and Liberation in a single lifetime. You, on the other hand, were born in a land where the noble doctrine of the Buddha prevails. Yet you have never listened to a single religious discourse, much less devoting your lives to a search for Truth."

Then, spontaneously, he sang a song about his many blessings–his hard mattress, his cotton quilt, his meditation band that held his knees in the proper position for samadhi, his disciplined body, his lucid mind, and his Final Goal.

"You have a marvelous voice, and the song is most inspiring," said one of the hunters. "I will remember it always."

A few weeks later, at the annual feast day in the village of Tsang-Tsa, some of those same hunters sang Milarepa's song. It happened that the hermit's sister, Peta, was there and heard the song and was moved by it. She said to the hunters, "The man who composed that song must be a very high soul–perhaps even a Buddha."

The hunters laughed and one said, "She has high praise for her own brother!"

Another said, "Buddha or brother, he is on the point of dying from starvation."

His sister Peta and Zesay come to his aid

Peta thought the men were joking with her and she began crying. At that point, by a remarkable coincidence, her cousin Zesay walked up and said, "You are Peta, are you not? I thought you had wandered away and died."

"I just came back," Peta said, "and I came to the feast to get some food. Now these men are making fun of me, saying my brother is nearby and is about to die of starvation."

"It could be true, Peta. I saw your brother some years ago. He told me he was going to spend the rest of his life meditating in the white rock cave on the other side of that mountain–" she pointed.

"Zesay! Will you go there with me? Oh, I wish I had some food to take to him!"

"There is enough food at this festival to satisfy a hundred hermits. Let's see how much we can pack away, and we'll go there!"

Taking as much chhang, bread, cheese and other food as they could carry from the copious supplies available at the feast, they set out for the white rock cave. When they got there, Milarepa was seated in meditation in the sunny glen outside his cave, and they were aghast to see that his eyes were sunken, his muscles reduced to thin cords, and his hair was stiff and filthy. But Peta ran and embraced him and begged him to partake of the beer and food. Over succeeding days both Peta and Zesay brought him more food and clothing.

After eating ample wholesome food for the first

time in many years, Milarepa went through a profound
change in consciousness. His chakras–psychic energy
centers–opened fully, giving him complete control of energy and mind. Now he had the power to change his form at
will, to transport himself instantly to any place on earth,
and to fly bodily in the air. Most important of all, he
enjoyed perpetually the blissful state of desirelessness.

Now an illumined adept, Milarepa's very existence
was a boon to humankind. People flocked to him. Over
succeeding decades he acquired thousands of followers,
including his sister Peta and his aunt. He gave hundreds
of sermons and discourses, and through his disciple
Rechung dictated a spirited autobiography to which all
who write about Milarepa are profoundly indebted.

At the age of eighty-four, Milarepa gave his final
discourse (on the law of karma) and distributed his
worldly possessions (a cotton loincloth and shirt, a skull
cap, flint and steel, a wooden bowl, a bone spoon and a
bamboo staff) to his close disciples. As he prepared for
mahasamadhi–the voluntary leaving of the physical
body–rainbows filled the sky, a heavenly fragrance
pervaded the air, and hosts of angels sang celestial hymns
for all who came to pay homage to Tibet's great yogi.

Rumi
(1207 -1273)

The gnat floats suspended in the bottle of wine.
No longer is it drunk, nor is it a gnat.
It is wine, pure wine.

–Jalaluddin Rumi

The thirteenth century was a time of strife, discord, persecution, and martyrdom. Amidst the corruption and chaos, mysticism was in flower in both the East and the West. This period was graced by the overlapping lives of three great lovers of God—Jalaluddin Rumi, Francis of Assisi and Meister Eckhart. At the time Rumi was born, Francis was twenty-five years old. And when Rumi died, sixty-six years later, Eckhart was a lad of thirteen.

Rumi had qualities in common with both of his great Christian contemporaries. In his early and middle years, he was, like Eckhart, an outstanding teacher, a bold intellect, and a respected theologian. In Rumi's later years, after divine love had been kindled in his heart, he turned his back on society and, like Francis, sought nothing as much as union with his Divine Beloved. Just as the love of Francis for Jesus was so overpowering that he eventually merged with the Christ in spirit, Rumi also achieved oneness with God through his master, Shams of Tabriz.

He was born in the city of Balkh, in what is now Afghanistan, to a family of scholars, judges, and Sufis. While he was still a child, his father, Professor Bahauddin Walad, found it politically expedient to pull up stakes and move his family out of the area after predicting (quite accurately) the Mongol invasion.

For the next sixteen years the family moved hither and yon, traveling through lands now known as Arabia, Syria, Armenia, Iran, Iraq and Turkey, while Genghis Khan and his horde swept through Afghanistan, Turkestan, and much of Persia, killing, burning, raping, and robbing. During their travels, Rumi's family made a pilgrimage to Mecca, visited Damascus and, in Nishapur, met the great Sheikh Fariduddin Attar, spiritual authority of that time, who blessed the young Rumi and gave him a copy of his book *Treatise on Mysteries*. Finally the family settled in Konya, in what is now southwest Turkey, where Professor Walad resumed his career of teaching theology.

Rumi was in his early twenties when his father died and left him an extensive library. The young man had already attracted considerable notice for his scholarship in jurisprudence, Islamic law and theology, and he succeeded to his father's teaching post.

A year or two later, Burhan al-Din Muhaqqiq, a Sufi adept and former student of Rumi's father, came to Konya in hope of seeing Professor Walad. A true dervish and perhaps an advanced soul, Burhan had reportedly reached heights of spiritual ecstasy while meditating in a remote mountainous region. When Burnhan learned that his revered teacher had died, he decided to devote his life to the spiritual training of his mentor's son Rumi. So, for nine years, he taught the precepts of Sufism to Rumi while the two traveled extensively. After his teacher died, Rumi returned to Konya to teach canonical law (*Shariat*) and theology.

Over the next five years Rumi was enormously successful. His lectures drew crowds in the hundreds, including many politically important people, such as sultans, princes, and viziers. According to his son, Sultan Walad (who later wrote a book about his father), Rumi had more than ten thousand followers at that time.

By all reports, Rumi was a conventional and

suitably pious teacher at that stage in his life. Known as
"the pillar of Shariat," he was a respectable family man.
(He was married twice —his first wife having died—and
he fathered four children.) But there is cause to suspect
that he was not altogether content within the walls of
orthodoxy--a reasonable assumption in view of his long
exposure to liberal Sufi teachings.

Everywhere were tensions and conflicts among
Muslims, Jews, Christians and Zoroastrians. It seemed that
most "religious" people either fostered the strife or were
oblivious to it. Rumi must have been uncomfortable with
popular points of view. Already he was pushing at the shell
of Shariat—expanding his inner horizons. None of his
contemporaries or disciples, however, could have
predicted the transformation that was soon to come.

In 1244 a wandering dervish called Shams-e Tabriz
(Shams of Tabriz) arrived in Konya. Shams wore an old
patched coat of wool and he had few worldly attachments
or possessions. When Rumi met Shams, he knew instantly
what had been missing in his life—and he knew he had
found it. In a tale he later wrote which is believed to refer
to his meeting with Shams, he said: "At sight of him, he
trembled, because love and awe are contrary to each other.
He saw those two contraries in his heart."

Shams threw Rumi's treasured books into a pool
and told him it was time for him to live what he had
learned. He ordered him to observe silence—to become
deaf to all external stimuli so that his inner senses could
function. As Rumi's son, Sultan Walad, later wrote: "The
great professor became a beginner in self-perfection."

Rumi stopped preaching and stopped teaching, cut
himself off from all social ties, and spent virtually every
moment with his master. Every day was a new learning
experience. Shams had many ways to teach his disciple
detachment and to purge his ego of concern for his
position and reputation in the community.

One day Shams ordered Rumi to fetch a large jug of wine from the local tavern. Since all alcoholic spirits were strictly forbidden to Muslims by religious law, it was not easy for a noted theologian (and professor of canonical law!) to buy a jug of wine and carry it on his shoulder through the streets of Konya. However, Rumi did it unflinchingly in response to his master's command.

Years later, in Rumi's major work *Diwan-e-Shams* (which contains 2,500 spontaneous odes with a meter that matches the heart beat), he wrote of Shams: "When he stimulated my thought from the depth of my psychic sea, the phantom of light arose. Shams was the light of the eye, the clarity of reason, the brightness of the soul, and the enlightenment of the heart. Shams was a universal man who took away my reason and religion. He was the form of every happiness."

The dervish and the professor became, in effect, a single soul inhabiting two bodies. Rumi was the earth revolving around the sun of Shams, who was the light of his life and the source of all energy and love. In the presence of Shams, he experienced ecstasy. Apart from him, he was a dead planet hurtling through the darkness of empty space.

But the academic and religious community of Konya, and especially Rumi's disciples, saw things very differently. To many of them, Shams was an interloper, a hypnotist, and quite possibly a fraud. The disciples no longer had access to their teacher, who now seemed unaware of their existence. Some said Rumi had clearly lost his mind and his reason. As Sultan Walad later wrote: "Why had our leader turned his back on us? We were all devoted followers who knew that he had no equal in either intelligence or understanding. He was the king of scholars and unexcelled as a teacher. Now he seemed lost, unaware of our existence. Who was this man who diverted our loving master from his chosen work?"

A plan was hatched. If Shams could be forced to leave town, Rumi's disciples reasoned, surely their teacher would return to his normal self. Opposition to Shams rose to such a height that observers predicted the dervish would be murdered or kidnaped. At this point, Shams left Konya and went to Damascus. But to the consternation of Rumi's disciples, their teacher did not "come back to his senses." His eyes were vacant and he seemed lost in a void. Hour after hour he circled a pole in his garden, searching for the center of his existence.

Finally, in desperation, Sultan Walad led a small group of Rumi's devotees in a search for Shams. When they found him in Damascus, they showered the dervish with gifts and homage and begged him to restore joy and sanity to their master. People lined the streets to watch as the procession returned to Konya. Shams-e Tabriz, in his tattered black coat, rode a white horse while Sultan Walad walked alongside, holding the stirrup of the steed.

With his master back, Rumi was in ecstasy, but the suspicion and jealousy increased. Two warring factions developed—those who were willing to tolerate Shams and accept Rumi as he had now become, and those who were even more determined to get rid of the dervish. A riot broke out, and men on each side, including one of Rumi's sons, were killed. During the fighting, Shams-e Tabriz disappeared without a trace—probably murdered. This was in 1248, when Rumi was forty-one.

For months the sorrowful Rumi circled the pole in his garden, whirling and twirling, while repeating constantly the name of God. In time, as his consciousness became more and more absorbed in the infinite, the dance of sorrow became a dance of joy and ecstasy. Rumi's dance, which became famous as the dance of the whirling dervishes, is symbolic of the search of the lover for the Divine Beloved, of the dispensation of God's grace to the aspirant, and of the divine theme of creation. With the con-

stant turning of the world, consciousness expands and
forms turn into higher forms, until eventually the seeker
becomes the Self he or she was seeking. The transmutation
of Rumi's ego-mind into the divine ego of his master took
about ten years to complete. And then, he experienced his
final change, transcending even his master. "I am not
Shams of Tabriz," he said. "I am pure light."

And he was love personified. Radiating bliss and
compassion, he lived in a state of spontaneous creativity.
Poems of great depth and beauty streamed from his lips,
and his disciples were kept busy transcribing the literally
thousands of poems and stories that are known to us today.

Here is my rendering of a Rumi poem.

I looked for him in churches and cathedrals.
    But no, he wasn't there.
I hunted him in the temples of Shiva, of Krishna, of Kali.
    But no sign of him did I find.
I searched the pagodas and peered into the eyes of the
    stone Buddha.
    There was no evidence he had been there.
I peeked into the mosques and minarettes of Islam,
    and kissed the sacred Kaaba.
    But no, he wasn't there either.
Finally I peered into my own heart,
    and there he was, hiding behind my desires.
He had been there all the time,
    and he was smiling at me.

Mirabai: Hindu Princess, Beggar and Saint
(1498 - 1549)

Beloved, I search the world for You,
hungry for Your love.
If it please You, Love, make my body a lamp,
and let my heart be the wick.
Fill that lamp with the nectar of my love,
Then let the lamp burn, and burn, and burn,
until the wick of my heart becomes ashes
at your precious lotus feet.
No longer can I bear the separation from You.
Make me Your own, Beloved;
make me One with You.
Make me love as You are love,
Beloved, Precious One!

–Mirabai

In the barren hills and ancient villages of
Rajasthan, in northwest India, time has little meaning.
Life goes on today in much the same manner as it did five
centuries ago, when Saint Mirabai was born. The bullock
carts still creak along the dusty roads. The farmers still
work their fields with wooden plows pulled by water
buffaloes. The women, dark-eyed and graceful, still draw
water from the same stone-rimmed wells and balance the
pitchers and pots on their heads as they swing along the
paths between fields of millet. And in the Mira Mandir, a
Krishna temple at Chitor built by Rajah Bhaj for the use of
his lovely *rani*, Mirabai, people still bow to Lord Krishna

and sing *bhajans* written by Mirabai for her Beloved.

Few Westerners have heard of Mirabai. In India, however, she is greatly revered for her beauty, her lovely songs, her devotion to God, and her life of selfless service. She was a queen who gave up wealth and position to worship God as she pleased–to wander, destitute, radiant in her rags. Mirabai was a lover of God whose faith was so great that a draught of poison given to her by her enemies turned to nectar on her lips. Her fame spread so widely during her lifetime that the Emperor Akbar, Moghul ruler of India, is said to have come in disguise to bow at her feet. For a Muslim leader to bow to any human being was heresy if not treason. And to bow to a female and a Hindu . . . !

Mirabai was born near the end of the fifteenth century, the only daughter of a Rajput prince killed soon thereafter in battle with the Moghul invaders of India. Known as Mira, she grew up in the palace of her uncle, who ruled the kingdom of Mewar.

One day the child saw a wedding procession. Her mother pointed out the lovely bride in her gold-brocaded sari and the resplendent bridegroom. Mira was enchanted. "Where is *my* bridegroom, Mother?" she asked.

Her mother smiled tenderly. "The Lord Krishna is your bridegroom, dear."

From that day onward, Mira considered herself to be the bride of Sri Krishna, the Avatar or God-man. According to Vedantic lore, the God-man takes a human body from time to time for the benefit of humanity. Although the man-form Krishna had lived thousands of years before Mira, she accepted him as her own personal Beloved. Soon after that, a wandering *sadhu* came to the palace and gave Mira a statuette of Lord Krishna. The child embraced the object and often danced and sang and prayed before the image.

Mira grew to be a beautiful young woman. At the

age of sixteen she was betrothed to Bhaj Raj, the crown
prince of Chitor. Before their wedding, Mira told him: "I
will be a loving and faithful wife to you. But you must
understand that Lord Krishna is my life and my eternal
Beloved."

Bhaj accepted without question Mira's devotion to
the Lord. "If I must share your love," he said, "let me share
it with the Highest of the High. For I could not share you
with any mortal man."

Soon after they were married, Bhaj's father died.
So Raj became the *rajah* (king) and Mira the *rani* (queen).
The change in station had no effect on Mira's religious
zeal. She continued to perform the ceremonies of *arti*,
puja, and *kirtan* before the statuette of Lord Krishna, and
to dance ecstatically for the pleasure of her Divine
Beloved.

Every day Mira visited the poor villagers of the
district, giving them food and comfort and teaching them
her love songs to Krishna. She prayed with the wandering
sadhus, dervishes and beggars, and chanted Krishna's
name wherever she went.

Although Bhaj remained tolerant of his wife's
spiritual fervor, his relatives were offended by her
behavior and tried to poison the king's mind against her.
Even the palace staff gossiped about the unconventional
rani. In an effort to quash the gossip, Bhaj built a special
temple for Mira's use. She accepted it lovingly and invited
all the sadhus and beggars to worship there with her, to the
mortification of her in-laws.

As time went on, songs and stories of Queen Mira's
beauty and saintliness were spread far and wide by
wandering ascetics and *bhaktas*. Spiritual seekers came in
droves to receive Mirabai's *darshan* (the blessing of her
presence) and to hear her sing her inspiring bhajans.

Then tragedy struck. King Bhaj, while leading his
troops against a Muslim army, was killed. Mirabai, at the

age of twenty-three, became the queen dowager. Her
brother-in-law, Ratan Singh, was crowned king of Chitor.

Ratan Singh and his wife had always been critical
of Mirabai. They felt that her public display of religiosity
was unseemly for a member of the royal household. The
most shocking thing was that she had refused to perform
the ancient rite of *suttee*–throwing herself on her dead
husband's funeral pyre. ("When the Divine Beloved wants
me," she said, "He can take me.") To add insult to injury,
she spent her bereavement not in seclusion but in the
company of her dervish friends, dancing and singing love
songs to Krishna.

In one of her song-poems, Mira wrote:

> *I embraced the hermits' company,*
> *and danced with them ecstatically.*
> *I chanted my sweet Krishna's name,*
> *while in-laws thought I was insane.*
> *They said I should have died by fire*
> *on my husband's funeral pyre.*
> *But my Beloved is not upset with me,*
> *so why, oh why, should Mira be?*

Unable to curb Mira's behavior by official means,
the king and queen plotted to kill her. They sent to her a
basket of flowers with a deadly cobra hidden inside. The
servant who delivered the gift told Mirabai it was a
shaligram (religious symbol). Mira accepted the gift
graciously, and when she raised the lid of the basket, there
was indeed a shaligram inside. Later she wrote:

> *After Mira danced and sang in public,*
> *the king sent her a snake in a basket.*
> *She prayed and bathed and looked inside*
> *to find her Beloved in brass.*

She also described other attempts on her life:

I know the king fed me poison,
but Krishna's grace saved me from harm

. . . .

. . . The queen sent a bed of spikes
for Mira to sleep upon.
When night fell and Mira slept,
she lay as though on feathers.

One story relates that Mirabai was ordered by the king to drown herself. She attempted dutifully to follow his instructions, but the river would not receive her. The waters rose and threw her back onto the bank.

Finally, in distress over the unhappiness at the palace caused by her ecstatic manner of worshipping God, Mirabai left Chitor and became a wanderer, singing of her love for Krishna wherever she went and attracting many devotees.

Upon reaching the holy city of Brindaban (where Krishna spent his childhood and where a thousand Krishna temples line the Jumna River), she is said to have taken the darshan of Swami Ramananda (guru of the great poet Kabir). Some scholars believe that Mira became Ramananda's disciple. Others point out that Ramananda probably died before Mirabai was born.

A story is told that Kabir once refused to speak at a spiritual conference because Mirabai (excluded evidently because of her sex) was not invited. A charming tale, but almost surely not true. According to reported dates, Mira was less than twenty years old when Kabir was well over a hundred.

Still other reports say that Mirabai was a disciple

of Tulsi Das, a well-known bhakta of northern India. Still others say that her guru was Raidas, a disciple of Ramananda, and that Raidas was the wandering sadhu who gave the statuette of Krishna to the child Mira.

After Mirabai's departure from Chitor, calamities befell the kingdom. The poor people, who loved Mira dearly, were almost in revolt against the king for his treatment of her. Even nature seemed to disapprove of the Chitor rajah, for serious illness struck his household, and the monsoon also failed, causing crop destruction. In desperation, the king repented for his persecution of Mira. In disguise, he made a pilgrimage to Mewar, where Mira had settled in her uncle's kingdom.

When the king and a group of accompanying Brahmins came into Mirabai's presence, they fell at her feet and begged her forgiveness, which she readily granted. But when they entreated her to return to Chitor, she told them she would have to ask the Lord Krishna for his counsel in the matter. Retiring to the temple for guidance, she prayed before a statue of Krishna. Legend says that the statue came alive and opened his arms to receive his loving bride, and the soul of Mirabai merged with her Divine Beloved.

Hafiz
(1320 - 1389)

Befitting a fortunate slave,
carry out every command of the Master
without any question of why or what.

About what you hear from the Master,
Never say it is wrong, because, my dear,
the fault lies in your own incapacity to
*   understand him.*

I am the slave of the Master who has released me
*   from ignorance.*
Whatever my Master does is of the highest benefit
*   to all concerned.*

–Hafiz, quoted by Meher Baba

Although no one is absolutely certain of the year
Persia's great poet Hafiz was born, most contemporary
writers (including A.J. Arberry, Paul Smith and Daniel
Ladinsky) fix the date at about 1320 A.D. This was about
sixty years after Baghdad was sacked and burned by
Hulagu, grandson of Genghis Khan, and some fifty years
after the death of the poet Jalaluddin Rumi.

Hafiz was born and lived and died in beautiful
Shiraz, a city that had miraculously escaped the looting,
raping and burning that blighted most of Persia during the
Mongol invasions of the thirteenth and fourteenth
centuries. At birth he was given the name Shamsuddin

Muhammad. The youngest of three sons, he grew up in a warm family atmosphere and, with his bright sense of humor and affectionate manner, was a joy to his parents, brothers and friends.

From childhood he showed an intense interest in poetry and religion. The name "Hafiz" signified both an academic degree in theology and an honorary title given to one who had memorized the entire Koran. In one of his poems, Hafiz tells us that he learned by heart fourteen different versions of the Koran.

When Hafiz was only about ten, his father died and left his widow in dire financial straits. Her two older sons left home to find work, while Hafiz and his mother moved in with his Uncle Saadi (a would-be poet who was named after the famous poet Saadi). A story is told that Uncle Saadi once left an unfinished ghazal on a table and came back to find that young Hafiz had completed the poem in sublime fashion, turning a bland and uninspiring fragment into a work of exquisite beauty. Saadi is said to have exclaimed that the poetry of Hafiz would cause madness in all who read it. High praise indeed since Uncle Saadi was no doubt referring to divine madness, or God-intoxication, an ecstatic condition that some, even today, believe can be the result of imbibing freely of the poetic outpourings of the winemaster Hafiz.

Because of the family's poverty, Hafiz's mother had to work outside the home, as did the boy Hafiz, whose salary paid his tuition at a night-school as well as helping with the family budget. Throughout his teen years he read avidly, studied diligently, learned calligraphy and began writing poems under his pen name "Hafiz."

He was twenty-one and employed at a bakery when one day he was asked to deliver bread to a prosperous section of town. While walking by a palatial home, his eyes met the lovely eyes of a young woman who stood watching him from a balcony. Hafiz was so smitten by the lady's beauty that he fell hopelessly in love with her.

The young woman was named Shakh-i-Nabat ("Wand of Sugarcane"), and Hafiz learned that she was engaged to be married to a prince. He knew, of course, that his love for her was hopeless, but that didn't stop him from writing poems about her. His poems were read and discussed in the wineshops of Shiraz and soon people all over the city, including the lady herself, knew of his passionate love for her.

Because of love, he attempts the impossible

Day and night Hafiz thought of the beautiful lady, and he could hardly sleep or eat. Suddenly one day he remembered a local legend about a Perfect Master, Baba Kuhi, who some three hundred years earlier had made a solemn promise that after his death anyone who could stay awake for forty consecutive nights at his tomb would receive the gift of immortal poetry, and also his heart's most fervent desire.

That very night, after finishing his work, Hafiz walked four miles out of town to the tomb of Baba Kuhi. He sat, stood and paced about the tomb all night long, pleading to Baba Kuhi for help in attaining his supreme desire—to obtain the hand and the love of the beautiful Shakh-i-Nabat.

Day after day, night after night, and week after week, he pursued his "impossible dream." Each morning he went to work at the bakery. In the evening, after work, he set out for Baba Kuhi's tomb. En route, as he passed the mansion where the love of his life resided, he once or twice saw her peeking at him through a window.

With each passing day, he became more gaunt and hollow-eyed. He moved and functioned like a man in a deep trance. Only his eyes were alive—like fiery coals. During his interminable nightly vigils he repeated, silently or aloud, the name of Baba Kuhi; but often, with a start, he would realize that the repetitions had changed, and he was now repeating the name of Shakh-i-Nabat! Chuckling to himself, he would beg the pardon of Baba Kuhi and go right on saying the lady's name.

By this time he had become convinced that Baba Kuhi understood and actually *approved* of his motivations; and in fact was helping him to accomplish his aims, nudging him awake when he was about to fall into deep sleep and planting ideas in his mind that helped him keep his tenuous grasp on reality and the difficult task at hand.

Finally, on the fortieth day, he walked to the shrine for the last night. As he passed the home of his beloved, she suddenly opened the door and came out to him. Throwing her arms around him, she told him between urgent kisses that she would rather be married to a genius than to a prince.

In an agony of desperation and desire, he tore himself away and, gasping out the name of Baba Kuhi, he hurried to meet his destiny at the tomb.

That fortieth night seemed endless. Yet, as dawn approached, a kind of power and exultation he had never known seemed to fill his being. He had succeeded! He had won. Soon he could claim his heart's desire!

With a roar like thunder and a light more brilliant than a thousand suns, a divine figure of matchless majesty appeared. The Angel Gabriel! The voice of Gabriel had the force of a hurricane and the rhythm of a great ocean wave, rising and falling and lifting and carrying Hafiz with it, higher and higher.

The Angel Gabriel told him that, through the grace of the Master of Love, the gift of immortal poetry was being bestowed on him. "And now," Gabriel intoned, "you may have one wish granted. Consider carefully. What is your heart's desire?"

Hafiz stared speechlessly at the most beautiful

being he had ever beheld. *If an angel of God can be that beautiful*, he thought, *what must Almighty God be like?* Finally he managed to say, "God. Yes, God! God is what I want!"

Gabriel smiled, and waves of color radiated across the sky. He told Hafiz that he should go to a certain shop in Shiraz, where the proprietor, a vendor by the name of Mohammed Attar, would be waiting for him.

Mohammed Attar was a God-realized soul, one of those rare Perfect Masters who work in secret, without public recognition. Attar embraced Hafiz and told him he had chosen wisely in asking for Godhood in preference to the many attractions of the world. Accepting Hafiz as one of his close disciples, he told him he must always keep his master's identity a secret. He also told him he must obey his orders implicitly. He should continue to write poetry and try to be patient. At the proper time, when he was ready, he would receive the prize of God-realization.

[We should note that Mohammed Attar was *not* the famous Perfect Master and poet Fariduddin Attar, who wrote *The Conference of the Birds* and other famous mystical works of twelfth century Persia.]

The successful forty-day vigil of Hafiz became widely known in Shiraz, making him something of a hero in the wineshops. But despite his deep experience of God and his initiation onto the spiritual path by his master, Hafiz still harbored a passionate love for Shakh-i-Nabat. Even though he later married another woman who bore him a son, the beauty of Shakh-i-Nabat would always inspire him as a reflection of the perfect beauty of God. After all, she, in a very real sense, was the impetus that drove him into the arms of his Divine Beloved, changing his life forever.

The poetry of Hafiz became well-known through-out Shiraz, and his fame and reputation grew. During the reign of Shah Abu Ishak, Hafiz was often invited to read his ghazals at court. The poet showed his gratitude by writing poems about Abu Ishak and about some of the shah's friends—judges, lawyers, professors, and an educator who founded a college and granted a professorship to Hafiz.

Somehow, while Hafiz was consorting with the rich and famous men of Abu Ishak's court, he fell deeply in debt. To avoid creditors, he left Shiraz and stayed in Yezd for two years. He returned secretly and remained hidden in a friend's house until some of his influential acquaintances worked out a settlement of his debts, which allowed him to resume his teaching post at the college.

Hafiz's first patron is beheaded

It wasn't long before the city of Shiraz was attacked and captured by the army of Mahommad ibn Muzaffar, whose first act was to close the wineshops where Hafiz's poetry was so popular. Later, by order of Muzaffar, Shah Abu Ishak, Hafiz's first official patron, was beheaded in the public square of Shiraz.

For a time Hafiz was sad and depressed, and his poetry revealed his state of gloom. He lost his job at the college and managed to survive by using his calligraphy talents. Then, to the astonishment of the whole city (and the gratification of many) the tyrannical Muzaffar was waylaid, blinded and imprisoned by his own son, Shudja. The new shah reopened the wineshops, for which he was praised in a Hafiz poem that was undoubtedly read with glee in all the wineshops in town. Hafiz now regained his teaching position, and was for a time in the good graces of the new ruler.

Biographer Paul Smith conjectures that this was a time when the poet's consciousness was being drawn inward by his master Mohammed Attar. The poetry of Hafiz became "spiritually impressionistic," or more subtle, Smith believes, because Hafiz was experiencing higher planes of consciousness. Smith's opinion seems to be supported by Meher Baba in his book *God Speaks,* which includes quotations from Hafiz to illustrate and clarify phenomena encountered by spiritual pilgrims while traversing higher planes of consciousness.

Shah Shudja, who himself knew the Koran by heart and also was a poet, soon became critical of some of the "impressionistic" poems of Hafiz, and he accused Hafiz of incoherence. At the same time, the conservative clergy, whose deceit and hypocrisy were highlighted in some of Hafiz's poems, began plotting against the poet. Regularly they railed against Hafiz at the shah's court, accusing him of slander and even blasphemy. Fortunately, one of the shah's closest advisors, Haji Kivam, was a strong defender of Hafiz.

Death of Hafiz supporter shows need to escape

But then, in 1362, Haji Kivam died and Hafiz no longer had a friend at court. Now the orthodox clergy increased their pressure on the shah to jail or deport Hafiz, and the poet made secret plans to move his wife and son out of Shiraz. But before the plans could be implemented, Hafiz's son suddenly became seriously ill and died. The poet's ghazals of the period demonstrate the intense grief that he and his wife suffered.

Soon the threat to Hafiz was lessened when Shiraz was invaded and Shudja deposed by the forces of Shah Mahmud, Shudja's own brother. Both Mahmud and his backer, the Sultan of Baghdad, greatly admired the ghazals of Hafiz, so now the poet's fame spread over all of Persia. The Sultan repeatedly invited him to come to Baghdad for an official visit, but Hafiz never accepted the invitations. One of his couplets, quoted by Paul Smith, expresses the poet's pleasure at staying home in Shiraz:

The breeze of Musalla's dust and the water of Ruknabad
Have never let me wander or ever travel too far away.

But stability and peace never lingered long in
Shiraz during the days of Hafiz. In 1366, Shudja returned
with a large, well-trained army and recaptured the city, and
Hafiz again feared for his life.

As pressures mounted, the poet went into hiding. In
the dead of night, he and his wife fled the city, beginning a
long, arduous journey of more than three hundred
miles to Isfahan, where they would spend the next four
long years. Many of Hafiz's ghazals written during that
period express his yearning for the sweet and bountiful
vale of Shiraz, where lived his master Mohammed Attar,
and also his beloved Shakh-i-Nabat.

In Isfahan, far from home and friends, Hafiz's
financial woes increased. Suddenly, like a gift from God,
he received a letter from the king of Bengal, in India.
The king told of a poignant personal situation involving
his health and three beautiful women in his harem, and of
his futile efforts to capture the drama of the situation in
verse. He had written the first line of a ghazal and simply
could not complete the poem. The best poets in India had
recommended Hafiz as the man who could do the job. In a
burst of inspiration, Hafiz completed the ghazal that very
day and sent it with his compliments to the king. For his
work, he received a gift of gold that allowed him to live
comfortably in Isfahan for several years.

But he still yearned for Shiraz. So Hafiz wrote a
letter to friends in the city, asking if he might safely come
home. It was now 1373 and Hafiz was fifty-three years
old, at the peak of his creative powers. Although he was
Persia's most famous poet, he was frustrated and often in
debt. It was difficult to earn money while in exile. To his
bitter disappointment, his friends wrote back to advise him
that the political climate in Shiraz was still volatile, and he

should stay away.

Next Hafiz wrote to friends in Yezd, who sent a
gracious invitation to him and his wife to come and stay
with them. So they traveled to Yezd, where they stayed for
another two years. While there, he read his ghazals at the
court of the Sultan of Yezd.

Then without warning, and to Hafiz's dismay, a
Yezd judge issued an advisory opinion that Hafiz should
be forcibly removed from Yezd and sent back to Shiraz.
However, by a fortunate coincidence, at the same time the
citizens of Shiraz petitioned Shah Shudja, clamoring for
the return of their famous native son, Hafiz. The shah,
against the wishes of the orthodox clergy, dispatched an
invitation to Hafiz, asking him to again honor the city of
Shiraz with his presence.

With great joy, Hafiz and his wife returned to
Shiraz in 1375, and he was again reinstated as a professor
at the college. Immediately, of course, he resumed his
close relationship with his spiritual master, Mohammed
Attar. It was during this period, in the view of Paul Smith,
that the poetry of Hafiz became "spiritually surrealistic."

Only a year after returning to Shiraz, Hafiz's wife
died. He wrote a ghazal lamenting that his "loved one was
torn from my arms by a malignant star." In his deep grief,
Hafiz begged his master to take him away from the pain of
the world and give him the union with God that he had
been promised, but Attar is said to have admonished Hafiz
for his lack of patience.

Soon after his wife's death, Hafiz received an invitation to visit King Bahmani, ruler of the Deccan Plateau
in India. The king was a lover of good poetry and was
willing to pay Hafiz well to make the long trip. Hafiz
requested an advance, and the king forwarded a generous
stipend. Hafiz gave some of his windfall to his creditors,
some to needy relatives, and kept the rest for travel costs.
Then, while en route to the Persian Gulf, he ran into a

friend who had been robbed by bandits, so the tender-
hearted Hafiz gave him all the rest of his money.

Two wealthy merchants who admired Hafiz's work
offered to pay his expenses for the remainder of the trip to
Bombay and overland to the Deccan Plateau. So they all
set off together and boarded a ship at Hurmuz. Before they
left port, though, a terrible storm came up, and Hafiz
concluded that God didn't want him to go to India after
all. So he wrote a special poem for the king and entrusted
it to someone on the ship to see that it was delivered. After
receiving the poem, the king was so pleased that he sent a
large sum of money to Hafiz for honoring him in verse
and for making an effort to visit his kingdom.

At long last, the prize of prizes
When he returned home, Hafiz vowed never to
leave Shiraz again, and he redoubled his efforts to obtain
the great prize he had been promised forty years earlier by
his master Mohammed Attar. In desperation, Hafiz is said
to have successfully completed the incredible trial known
as *Chehel-a-Nashini,* in which an aspirant sits within a
circle drawn on the ground for forty days and nights
without leaving the circle. After that accomplishment by
his disciple, the master Attar ceremoniously served a drink
of red wine to Hafiz and bestowed on him the eternal gift
of God-realization.

During the remaining eight years of his life, Hafiz
composed almost as many poems as he had heretofore
written in his whole lifetime. No longer did he write of the
agonies of separation from the Beloved. No longer did he
write as the lovesick lover seeking the pleasure of his lady.
Now he wrote of the stages of the Spiritual Path, which he
had personally traversed, and of the unity of God, which he
now experienced.

Some of the ecstasy of the later ghazals of Hafiz is
imparted in the marvelous renderings of Daniel Ladinsky

in his book, *The Subject Tonight Is Love.*The following lines are from one of Ladinsky's longer renderings, titled "Like the Ganges."

I ecstatically speak with words and also with
The purest language–Silence–

Saying in a thousand different ways:

"Dear countrymen, and all my nearby cousins–
Comets and galaxies,

Every amoeba, creature and plant,
Bring your cup and I will pour you God.
O, when the Friend begins to sway
From being so full of love,

Music flows like the Ganges from
My mouth."

Another rendering of Hafiz by Ladinsky is called "A Potted Plant."

I pull a sun from my coin purse each day.
And at night I let my pet the moon
Run freely into the sky meadow.

If I whistled,
She would turn her head and look at me.

If I then waved my arms,
She would come back wagging a marvelous tail
Of stars.

There are always a few men like me
In this world

Who are house-sitting for God.
We share His royal duties:

I water each day a favorite potted plant
Of His–this earth.

Ask the Friend for love.
Ask Him again.

For I have learned that every heart will get
What it prays for
Most.

One more exquisite rendering of Hafiz by Daniel Ladinsky is called "Why All This Talk?"

Why all this talk of the Beloved,
Music and dancing,
And liquid ruby-light we can lift in a cup?

Because it is low tide,
A very low tide in this age
And around most hearts.

We are exquisite coral reefs,
Dying when exposed to the air
And to strange elements.

God is the wine-ocean we crave–
We miss
Flowing in and out of our pores.

We cannot close the story of Hafiz without relating an oft-told anecdote about the fearsome conqueror Tamerlane (Timur the Lame), who laid to waste much of Persia and entered Shiraz after slaughtering an estimated seventy thousand citizens of Isfahan and making a huge pyramid of their bloody heads.

Years before Tamerlane's arrival, he had captured the cities of Bokhara and Samarkand and had made them his twin capitals. At that time, Hafiz had written a poem poking fun at the conquests of Tamerlane.

Belle of Shiraz, grant me but love's demand,
And for your mole, that clinging grain of sand
Upon a cheek of pearl, Hafiz would give
All of Bokhara and Samarkand.

Tamerlane had heard about the poem, and he never forgot it. After Shiraz capitulated without a fight, and his troops marched triumphantly into the city, Tamerlane sent out his tax men to collect indemnity from each citizen (his reward for not slaughtering them.) When the collector came to the house of Hafiz, the poet pleaded indigence and said he could not make a contribution.

After being told that Persia's celebrated poet had not paid tribute, Tamerlane angrily issued a warrant of arrest. The next day Hafiz, shabby and unkempt, stood before the throne of the fierce monarch.

Leaning forward to scowl at Hafiz, Tamerlane said, "Do you know who I am?"

"Yes, your excellency," replied Hafiz courteously. "You are the great Tamerlane."

"Indeed I am," sneered Tamerlane. "And you, I believe, are a poet of some repute." He threw his head back and looked down his nose at Hafiz. "I have been told that you once composed a verse about the high value you assign to a mole on your mistress's cheek. Are you the one who wrote that silly verse that made me the laughingstock of the world? Did you write that tripe?"

Hafiz shrugged. "I'm afraid so, your excellency."

Tamerlane drew himself up. "With the blows of my silver sword, I have subdued a quarter of the inhabited world. I have burned and leveled thousands of towns and cities–all to enrich my capital cities of Bokhara and Samarkand. And yet *you!*" he jabbed a massive finger at Hafiz, "*you, pitiful one, would trade my cities for the mole on the cheek of your mistress!*"

Shrugging again, Hafiz said softly, "It is because of such extravagant generosity on my part that you see me today in such a miserable and pitiable condition."

Roaring with laughter, Tamerlane told the poet to go in peace. The wit of Hafiz had saved the day.

In 1389, after composing his own obituary, Hafiz laid down his mortal frame. But even in death, he was the center of controversy. While his followers and close friends carried his body to the Muslim burial ground on the banks of his beloved Ruknabad River, some of the orthodox clergy, claiming that the poetry of Hafiz was blasphemous, denied permission to bury his body on hallowed ground.

An argument ensued and someone suggested they consult the works of Hafiz to seek an answer to the dilemma. Hundreds of Hafiz's poems were cut into couplets and placed in a pot. A child was chosen to draw out a single strip of paper. The couplet selected read:

Never abandon the bier of Hafiz.
Although immersed in sin, he dwells in Paradise.

Again, the indomitable Hafiz had the last word. Shouting with joy, his friends lifted the bier on which his body lay and carried it to the gravesite, at the base of a cypress tree that Hafiz himself had planted. Inscribed on the beautiful tomb that was later built are the words:

When you pass the bier of Hafiz, ask for grace,
For it will be a place of pilgrimage for the profligates
*   of the world.*

Even today, many spiritual aspirants use the *Divan of Hafiz* as an oracle, going to it for answers just as many Christians and Jews consult the Holy Bible. In the Islamic world, Hafiz is widely accepted as a spiritual master and one of the premier poets of all time. In the western world, the richness and beauty of his words, and the contagious quality of the love and light expressed, are appreciated more and more by seekers and lovers of God who find inspiration and joy in the new interpretations of his ghazals that reach us today.

Kabir
(1390 - 1517)

Benares to the East,
Mecca to the West.
Explore the heart within you, friend.
Both Ram and Allah are there.

. . . .

Where do you seek Me?
Lo, I am beside you.
I am not in outer rites and ceremonies;
I am by you, with you, within you!

–Kabir

Around the end of the fourteenth century, in the holy city of Benares, a Muslim weaver and his wife found a newborn baby in a bed of lotuses at the edge of the Ganges River. According to the story, the baby greeted the couple by saying "*Ba-ba,*" which means God, or Father. The couple, who had no children, accepted the child as a gift from Allah, and were not bothered by the fact that the baby was probably of Hindu blood. They named him Kabir, which means "Great One."

Benares is predominantly Hindu, so Kabir was raised in a minority class, but a class that then ruled India. From his earliest days, the boy was creative, energetic, and spiritually inclined. Following in the footsteps of his foster father, he became a weaver.

While still a youth, Kabir determined to become a disciple of the well known Hindu Sadguru Ramananda.

Kabir's family and friends tried to dissuade him. "Swami Ramananda will never accept a Muslim disciple," they said. "Be patient. When the time is ripe, and it is Allah's will, you will find yourself a Muslim teacher. That will be better for all concerned."

But Kabir was not to be diverted from his goal. Somehow he felt that he was destined to be a disciple of Ramananda. So he laid his plans carefully, and early one morning he went to the bathing ghats on the River Ganges where Ramananda bathed and greeted the sun each day. Hiding in a dark shadow beneath one of the huge stone steps, he waited, and when Swami Ramananda descended toward the river, the guru stepped on the youth and cried out, "Ram! Ram!"

Kabir prostrated himself before the sadguru and said, "Thank you, my master. I am your obedient servant."

"What's this? Why should you call me your master, young man? Who are you?"

Kabir looked up and held his hands together in the typically Hindu manner of greeting. "I am your devoted slave, my master."

"How did I become your master when I have never seen you before?" Ramananda demanded.

"But, Master," Kabir said softly, "You initiated me. You gave me a mantra, 'Ram, Ram.'"

Ramananda smiled and put his hand on the youth's head. "*Ah cha*! You are a very clever lad. Accept those words as your mantra, and repeat them constantly. Devote your life to the service of others. See God in all, give Him your complete obedience, and you will realize Him." In that way Kabir became a *chela* of Swami Ramananda, and eventually his closest disciple and successor.

Kabir often referred to himself as a child of both Ram and Allah. He respected all paths to God, but had no use for the outer trappings of religion. A family man with many children, he remained a simple, direct man who saw

no need for asceticism, mortification of the flesh, nor
excessive piety.

"God is both within and without," he said.
Therefore, what need is there to hold your breath, contort
your body, perform rituals or go on pilgrimages to sacred
places? "In love, appearances do not matter," he said. "If
you wish, live in a house. If you'd rather, dwell in the
forest. It makes no difference."

Here is my rendering of a well known Kabir poem.

The sacred bathing places are fine for taking a bath.
But take Kabir's advice and bathe at home. It's cheaper.
And it's okay to go to shrines and see the idols
        and graven images.
Some of them are beautiful art, but they can't speak to you
        or open the doorway to your heart.
The Koran and Upanishads are mere words, nothing more.
What do you seek? A clean body, a stone statue, a bunch
        of words or the One?
Listen! His hiding place is closer than you think.

Such ideas are likely to raise the ire of most clerics
and religious teachers, so Kabir was often persecuted.
Once, hostile Brahmin priests sent a courtesan to tempt
Kabir, and she, like Mary Magdelene, was converted to a
higher love.

A story is told about a leper who touched the arm
of Kabir and was instantly healed, and he went about
shouting that Kabir was God in human form. Brahmins
who were hostile to Kabir seized on the incident to file a
complaint with the Muslim emperor, Sikander Lodi. The
Brahmins were sure that any Muslim ruler would be
infuriated by the report that a mere man was reputed to be
God. In deference to the priests, the emperor banished
Kabir from Benares, but his life was spared. (According to
another version of the story, Kabir was sentenced to be

trampled by an elephant, but the animal, apparently frightened by an angelic apparition standing in its path, refused to
step on Kabir.)

Nowadays, Kabir is claimed by both Muslims and
Hindus, and even during his lifetime he had disciples from
both camps. Legend has it that, when Kabir announced
his approaching death (reportedly at the age of over 100)
an argument broke out among his disciples. The Hindus
wanted to cremate their master's body, while the Muslims
wanted to bury it. But after Kabir passed away, no body
was found in his bed—only a mass of fragrant flowers. So
the Hindu contingent cremated half the flowers, while the
Muslims buried the other half.

The tale may well be apocryphal, but this much is
true. Today, at Magar, two Kabir tombs exist. One tomb is
claimed by the Muslims to be the final resting place of
their master, and the other is claimed by the Hindus to be
the spot where Kabir's ashes are buried.

Perhaps a million people in India today accept
Kabir as their spiritual master. But in the West, Kabir is
better known as a great mystical poet whose works are in
the tradition of Rumi, Hafiz, and other great Sufi poets
who were also spiritual masters. The following poems contain the essence of the life and teachings of Kabir, and
exemplify the joy of the path to God through the heart.

> *Nothing I have belongs to me.*
> *All that I have belongs to You.*
> *What will I lose if I surrender to You*
> *What belongs to You?*
> —(translated by Meher Baba)

The next is my own rendering of a Kabir poem
translated by Linda Hess and Shukdev Singh, and
published on the Internet.

The world is mad as a hatter.
When I tell the truth, they want to kill me.
If I lied, they'd run after me with praise.

I've seen the pious Brahmins worshipping rocks;
the Muslims bowing to a black cube far away.
Posturing yogis, oozing pride,
painting their brows, twisting their limbs,
chanting their mantras in the streets.

Hindus say Ram is the Beloved;
Muslims say Allah is the One.
They both love God, but they kill each other.
No one seems to know the secret.

Kabir says, listen seekers and saints,
It's so simple that nobody gets the point.

One of my favorites is based on a translation by
Tagore:

Since the day I first met my Lord,
there has been no end to the sport of our love.
I don't need to shut my eyes, or close my ears,
or torture myself.
I see with eyes open and I smile and behold
His beauty wherever I look.

I repeat his Name, and look around me,
and everything reminds me of Him;
Whatever I do, it becomes His worship;
The food I eat is His prasad.
The rising and sinking of the sun
are the same to me.

All problems are resolved.
Wherever I go, I find Him there;
He precedes, follows and accompanies me.

All I achieve is His gift.
When I lie down, I lie at His feet.
He is the only adorable One in existence.
There is no other.

My tongue sings His glory day and night.
Whether I rise or sit down,
I can never forget Him,
for the rhythm of His music beats in my ears.

Kabir says: "My heart is afire,
and my soul is aglow.
I am drowning in the bliss
that transcends all pleasure and pain."

Teresa of Avila
(1515 - 1582)

Over four hundred years ago, not long after Columbus made his historic voyages to the New World, and while Mirabai in India was singing her songs of love for Krishna, another female saint lived in Spain. Like Mirabai, Teresa experienced ecstatic visions and was often aflame with love for God. Teresa, however, did not openly display her love for her Beloved. While Mirabai sang and danced in the streets, Teresa lived in a convent, where behavior was strictly monitored and displays of passion (even if directed to the Lord) were severely frowned upon. India in the sixteenth century was imbued with the free spirit of *bhakti*, while Spain was enduring the paranoia of the Inquisition.

It was a time when a young Spanish woman of good breeding had only two real choices: to marry and raise a family or go into a convent. All aspects of life were controlled by the Church, and the Inquisition enforced conformity with the very real threat of torture and death. After seven centuries of Arab occupation of Spain, the last of the Moors had been driven out of the country—in the year 1492. With the Muslim threat finally eradicated, the king and queen, Ferdinand and Isabella (who sent Christopher Columbus on his famous expeditions to the Americas) issued an edict banishing all Jews. The only way Jewish people could remain in Spain was to disavow Judaism and convert to Christianity.

In recent decades, evidence has come to light suggesting that Teresa was of Jewish blood, and that her family became Catholics to escape persecution and expulsion. These facts, if true, only make Teresa's story even more remarkable.

Teresa of Avila (who took the name Teresa of Jesus as a nun) was a most remarkable person. Even if you disregard her sainthood and her spiritual experiences, she was still brilliant and fascinating in the worldly sense. Headstrong, witty, vivacious, and charming, she knew how to get her way, and how to get things done. She had a strong artistic bent and was a talented writer, a superb organizer and an innovator. Always a practical woman, she somehow found time to carry on an ardent love affair with Jesus Christ that lasted for decades and produced some of the world's greatest mystical literature.

She was born on March 28, 1515, one of the nine children of Don Alonso Sanchez y Cepeda and his wife Donna Beatriz. When she was only about seven, she and her eleven-year-old brother Rodrigo read the classic work *Lives of Saints* together. They were enchanted to read in the book that the bliss from God-consciousness was "everlasting." Teresa and Rodrigo took to repeating the words, "For ever, ever, ever," and the repetition produced positive effects on her consciousness. "Through the constant uttering of these words," she wrote in her *Life* (her spiritual autobiography), "our Lord was pleased that I should receive an abiding impression of the way of truth when I was yet a child."

Seeking martyrdom at age seven

When the children read of Christian martyrs being beheaded by the Muslims, Teresa states that "I had a great desire to die a martyr's death—not out of any love of Him of which I was conscious, but that I might most quickly attain to the fruition of those great joys of which I read that they were reserved in Heaven; and I used to discuss with my brother how we could become martyrs."

So the two children, one seven and one eleven, made plans to run away from home, to travel by "begging

our way for the love of God," and somehow to cross the
Straits of Gibraltar to the land of the Moors, where they
would surely be beheaded (they believed), and thereby be
taken straight to Heaven.

They actually put their plan into motion, slipping
out of the house and leaving the city by way of the Adaja
Gate. After they crossed the bridge outside the city limits,
they were spotted by their uncle, who brought them home.
Their mother had already been all over Avila searching for
them. When questioned about their plans, the children
confessed everything, and Rodrigo claimed it was not his
fault at all, but his little sister had talked him into it.

As an adolescent girl, Teresa avidly read stories of
romance and chivalry, a habit picked up from her mother.
She was thirteen years old when her mother died. In her
Life, she tells how she went weeping to a statue of the
Virgin Mary in the Avila Cathedral (where the statue still
stands) and begged Mary to be her mother. It is possible
that her mother's sad life and many difficult pregnancies
played a part in Teresa's later decision to become a nun.

She commits a "mortal sin"

As a teenager, Teresa was outgoing and popular.
When she was fifteen or sixteen, she was led into some
sort of forbidden behavior by a female cousin and another
unnamed person. While "blinded by passion," she says,
she committed a "mortal sin." As a result, at the age of
sixteen, she was placed by her father in an Augustinian
convent, Our Lady of Grace, which was a kind of
boarding school for daughters of affluent families.

Teresa adapted quite well to the cloistered life, but
she had no interest in making a career of it. In fact, she
tells us, she was "most hostile to being a nun." However,
by the time she became ill after eighteen months and was
sent home, she had begun to give serious consideration to
the prospect.

This was not due to any lofty aspirations, she assures us, but purely from her fear of Hell. Because her health was so bad, she was afraid she would die without having attained the state of Grace that convent life was supposed to produce. Her attitude was much the same as she had displayed at age seven. She wanted to get on the "fast track" to Salvation.

Several years later, when she was about twenty, she decided definitely to enter the Carmelite Convent of the Incarnation in Avila. Her father objected, however, and refused to give his permission. So in 1536 she ran away for the second time. And again, she talked one of her brothers into leaving with her—he to go into a nearby monastery while she went into the Incarnation. They slipped out of the house before dawn, and when Teresa reached the convent, the prioress dispatched a messenger to Don Alonso, who immediately gave his consent to his daughter's becoming a nun.

At the brink of death

Before she had been long at the convent, Teresa became gravely ill. We are not sure of the exact nature of her disease (which gives fuel to those writers who classify Teresa as a hysterical, epileptic, and sexually frustrated woman), but she writes of her frequent heart attacks, fainting spells, high fever, intense pain, inability to eat, weight loss, and insomnia.

Physicians who were sent to the convent by her father concluded that she was dying of consumption and there was nothing they could do. Teresa was carried home to die. And die she did, in the judgment of her attending physicians. When she suddenly revived after four days in a deep coma, preparations for burial had been made, and a contingent of nuns had been sent to get the body. Teresa awoke to find her eyes had already been sealed with wax, as was the custom of the day.

Teresa's description of her condition at that time is grim. She had bitten her tongue "to pieces," her bones all seemed out of joint, and her whole body was bruised and swollen. (These symptoms, of course, suggest epileptic seizures or convulsions.)

Partially paralyzed for three years

She was carried back to the convent, where she remained partly paralyzed for about three years. She considered herself greatly improved when she was able to move about on her hands and knees! But eventually she recovered and was able to assume the regular duties of a nun. Which were not at all rigorous or austere, in those days. Most Carmelite convents of that period, including the Incarnation, operated under the relaxed "mitigated" rule. Nuns were permitted to wear jewelry and makeup, to keep pets, to entertain visitors of either sex in the parlor, and to obtain special permission to leave the convent almost at will. As we might suspect, there were many tales of improper and scandalous conduct by nuns as well as priests. It was because of "too much freedom" in the Carmelite convents of that time that Teresa, many years later, instituted her much-needed reforms.

As the years went by, Teresa's health gradually improved. The "raptures" and ecstatic trances that later became a regular part of her life apparently improved her health also. At least, she believed so. She discovered, she tells us in her autobiography, that the less attention she paid to her body and its ailments, the better she felt. (Does this sound like a hysterical personality?)

Even though Teresa was the recipient of special "graces" from the Lord after only a short period in the convent, for about twenty years she often was torn between God and the world. During one difficult period she actually went for a whole year without praying! Every day in the periods set aside for prayer and contemplation, she only pretended, she tells us, while her mind was meditating on the hour-glass!

Anyone who reads Teresa's books is bound to be grateful for her candor and honesty. We are disappointed, though, when she attributes her weaknesses to her being a member of the weaker sex. We must remember, however, that all her books were written under the direct orders of her confessors and advisors, all of whom were men. In her numerous self-deprecatory statements, and her remarks about the failures and stupidities of women in general, she is probably reflecting the opinions of the strictly male hierarchy of the Catholic Church, which of course had the power at all times to denounce her to the Inquisition.

Years of bitter pain followed by exquisite bliss

Her first twenty years in the convent, Teresa says, were "the most painful life that can be imagined, because I had no sweetness in God and no pleasure in the world." But finally she worked her way through that extremely difficult period and began to have ecstatic visions in which Christ often spoke to her and sometimes even appeared to her. She had incredible experiences of "union" with the Divine Beloved; blissful states in which her body became cold, cataleptic, and apparently lifeless. Many of these states may well have been identical to the higher *samadhi* of the yogis. She often had intense "raptures" in which her body would actually levitate. These raptures were particularly bothersome to her when they occurred in the presence of others, since they caused no end of talk.

One levitation occurred during a mass on the Feast of St. Joseph, with many "great ladies" and other guests present. Teresa was kneeling when she felt it coming on, so she seized an iron grating to try to hold herself down. This was after she had become Prioress of the Incarnation, and her nuns clustered around her to try to keep her from becoming a spectacle; but despite all efforts to restrain her,

her body rose into the air in the full view of the Bishop of Avila, who was saying the mass.

In later years, after John of the Cross became Teresa's friend and spiritual advisor, the two saints, while conversing in the parlor at the Incarnation, reportedly were seen levitating simultaneously.

But until that happy period when she finally had a confidant and confessor who understood what she was going through, Teresa's visions and "locutions" caused her great anguish. At first she thought she might have been deceived by Satan; but since each experience magnified her love for God and strengthened her inner conviction that God was doing it all, her doubts were overcome. Usually, however, when she described her experiences to her advisors and confessors, they refused to believe that God would give such graces to anyone as sinful as Teresa admitted herself to be.

They declared emphatically that Teresa was being deluded by Satan. She was advised to always make the sign of the cross when such "apparitions" occurred, and furthermore to show her disdain for any manifestation or vision by "giving it the finger," a contemptuous gesture that is still employed today as a display of vulgarity, but hopefully not by saints and other sincere seekers! Teresa tells us that when she followed her confessors' advice, the visions became even more convincing, and she felt even more bliss.

Eventually, of course, Teresa realized that she knew much more about the spiritual path than did her confessors. And having taken a vow of obedience, she was in a terrible quandary. Should she "give the finger" to Jesus Christ just because her advisors, out of ignorance, ordered her to? To solve this conundrum, she went to Jesus for advice, and He told her she should always obey her superiors as she had vowed to do. However, He said, He would guide her in all future conversations with her confessors, and she was not to worry because He would see that the situation would soon improve.

Things did indeed get better. A real man of God, and a true saint, Peter of Alcantara, came into Teresa's life and gave her much helpful advice and companionship. They remained friends for the rest of his life, and beyond, for even after Peter's death he frequently appeared to her, offering advice and counsel to her during the next twenty years, until she too left this world.

In her *Life*, Teresa reveals her no-nonsense, common sense approach to spirituality. No matter how much we may desire God, she says, we should not neglect the body. We must eat regularly and get exercise ("Go out in the fields"). We should not neglect our friends and co-aspirants, and we should spend part of every day in "enjoyable conversation" with others.

Meditation is important, but practicing the presence of Christ in our everyday life is even more important. Her remarks on that subject remind us of Brother Lawrence, a Carmelite lay monk in France who came along about a hundred years after Teresa and built his life around practicing the presence of God. Teresa also spoke of finding God in the kitchen among the pots and pans—which is another practice that is generally attributed to Brother Lawrence.

Teresa wrote: "The soul may also place itself in the presence of Christ, and accustom itself to many acts of love directed to His sacred Humanity, and remain in His presence continually, and speak to Him, pray to Him in its necessities, and complain to Him of its troubles; be merry with Him in its joys, and yet not forget Him because of its joys. All this it may do without set prayers, but rather with words befitting its desires and its need.

"This is an excellent way whereby to advance, and that very quickly. . . .This practice of the presence of Christ is profitable in all states of prayer, and is a most

safe way of advancing to the first state, and of attaining
quickly to the second; and as for the last states, it secures
us against those risks which the devil may occasion."

Her plan to reform the convents

The longer Teresa stayed in the Incarnation, the
more she felt that the structure of the Church was being
undermined by sloth, lust and high living. Christ had
instilled in her the desire to establish a convent that would
follow the "primitive" rules of the original Carmelite order
that lived by Mount Carmel, in Lebanon, in the twelfth
century. Teresa's dream was to set up a convent of
"barefooted Carmelites" to operate free of the need for
public endowments.

Nuns would have no luxuries and few of the
freedoms allowed at the Incarnation. The emphasis would
be on prayer and contemplation. Any female who was
sincerely interested in finding God would be admitted
regardless of her resources or station in life. (Under the
entrenched "mitigated" rule, convents often accepted only
girls who could pay a sizable dowry.)

Teresa knew of the many obstacles to be faced, and
the strong opposition she could expect from the Church
hierarchy, not to mention the thousands of nuns who
enjoyed the freedoms they had been given. The few
persons she spoke to about her plan agreed it was a good
idea in concept, but it wouldn't work. It wasn't practical.
How could you run a convent without an endowment?

When Teresa became discouraged and was about to
abandon the plan, Christ spoke to her clearly and firmly
and commanded her to go ahead with it. He would see that
she succeeded, He assured her.

At about this time, her two great friends and fellow
saints, John of the Cross and Peter of Alcantara, offered
their support and urged her to go ahead. This she did,
working in secret because there was grave danger that her

immediate superiors would forbid her to proceed if they knew about her plans. Many at the Incarnation knew what she was doing, however, and much ill-feeling developed.

"I was now very much disliked throughout the whole convent," she wrote, "because I wished to found another with stricter enclosure. It was said I insulted my sisters; that I could serve God among them as well as elsewhere, for there were many among them much better than I; that I did not love the house, and that it would have been better if I had procured greater resources for it than for another. Some said I ought to be put in prison; others– but they were not many–defended me in some degree. I saw well enough that they were for the most part right, and now and then I made excuses for myself; thought as I could not tell them the chief reason, which was the commandment of the Lord, I knew not what to do, and so was silent."

Christ turns the key

Finally, almost miraculously (and through divine intervention, Teresa believed), she obtained the approval of the Provincial, who was in charge of all religious houses in the province. At about the same time, a high-ranking lady, Dona Luisa de la Corda, sister of a duke and widow of a close relative of the Archbishop, needed spiritual guidance and asked the Provincial to delegate Teresa to move into the lady's home and counsel her.

During the following months Teresa had the freedom to work unhampered on the development of the new facility. But then the citizens of Avila raised a loud protest. They were offended by the thought of having to support a group of penniless nuns who were trying to live off the land.

But somehow it all came together, and it worked. Teresa opened the monastery and convent of St. Joseph. The rules were strict, in line with the rules of the original

Carmelites. Fasting was re-introduced, as well as modified vegetarianism. Fish and fowl were eaten, but not red meat. Nuns wore a coarse habit without jewelry, and took vows of chastity, poverty, seclusion, enclosure and silence. They lived on donations and whatever they could earn by spinning, weaving, gardening and crafts. They were not really barefoot, but wore plain sandals woven of rope. Except for hours set aside for silence, meditation and prayer, the nuns enjoyed songs, spiritual dancing, poetry and story-telling.

After St. Joseph was successfully established, Teresa went on to reform many convents and also set up seventeen new ones, which were designed as true models for the community of what cloistered living should be. In doing this work, Teresa traveled a great deal, over bad roads in uncomfortable carriages, staying in dirty inns often filled with vulgar people. Reforms never come easy, especially when dealing with the male-dominated Catholic Church. But Teresa was an able politician, with great powers of persuasion. One of her confessors once said: "Good Lord! I would rather deal with all the theologians in creation than with that woman!"

Years later she was ordered to return to the Incarnation as the Prioress. This caused consternation and commotion among the nuns of the Incarnation. And Teresa, as well, did not want the job of taking charge of the same nuns she had lived with and worked with for twenty-five years. She had no choice in the matter, however, and she acquitted herself so well that all the nuns in her charge grew to love, and even revere, her.

But even Teresa did not succeed in reforming her own convent! The Incarnation did not accept Teresa's Carmelite Reform until 1940! Today, however, the nuns at the Incarnation live austere lives of joy and creativity. Our dear friends Jane Haynes (now deceased) and her son Charles have visited the Incarnation many times and have told us that the spirit of Teresa and her great love for Christ is very much alive there today.

Christ gives her assignments in the world

In later years, when Teresa had great influence, Christ often told her to go see a particular person and tell him thus and so. Sometimes Teresa objected strenuously to such orders on the part of her Lord. Once she said, in effect, "Why me, Lord? Can't You speak directly to the man? Why give me such a difficult mission?" The Lord replied, "Since you can't do great things for Me, I'd like you at least to help others to serve Me. Besides, the man is not disposed to prayer and would not believe Me if I spoke to him."

Another time Teresa said: "Lord, are there not others—for instance, theologians—who would carry out this mission better than I, a wretched sinner, if Thou would but speak to them?"

Christ answered: "Theologians will do nothing to enter into personal communication with Me. Repulsed by them, I must choose women to open to them My heart and speak of My affairs."

Once when the Lord had told her to go and reform the monastery of Paterna in 1575, and she dreaded it and was distressed about it, the Lord said: "What art thou afraid of? What canst thou lose? Only thy life, which thou hast so often offered to Me. I will help thee."

In her autobiography, Teresa tells the touching story of how Christ sent an angel to open her heart. This was in 1559, when she was forty-four years old. She wrote:

"I saw in his hand a long spear of gold, and at the iron's point there seemed to be a little fire. He appeared to be thrusting it at times into my heart, and to pierce my very entrails; when he drew it out, he seemed to draw them out also, and leave me all on fire with a great love of

God. The pain was so great that it made me moan; and yet so surpassing was the sweetness of this excessive pain that I could not wish to be rid of it. The soul is satisfied now with nothing less than God. The pain is not bodily, but spiritual . . . . It is a caressing of love so sweet which now takes place between the soul and God, that I pray God of His goodness to make him experience it who may think that I am lying.

"During the days that this lasted I went about as if beside myself. I wished to see or speak with no one, but only to cherish my pain, which was to me a greater bliss than all created things could give me."

Teresa died in 1582 at the age of 68. She departed in a state of bliss, seeing the Christ before her and eager to join her Divine Beloved.

George Fox and the Inner Light
(1624 - 1688)

The seventeenth century in England was a time of religious unrest, ferment, and persecution. After England rejected Catholicism to allow King Henry VIII to divorce his wives, the Church of England came under fire from the Puritans, who set out to "purify" the Church. A civil war was fought between the Puritans and the Royalists, and the resulting reforms were harsh and intolerant. Laws were enacted that meted out cruel punishments to persons convicted of blasphemy.

This was the age of George Fox, a great lover of God who was guided solely by the voice of God speaking within his heart. He never had a human master, nor even a teacher he could accept. From the time he began preaching of the "light within," George Fox was battered, beaten, insulted, slandered, ridiculed, and imprisoned. But he was never defeated, and he never backed down. He shook the empire and the religious establishment, and he started a great mystical movement, the Quakers, that gained much-deserved respect even during his lifetime.

Born in 1624, George Fox grew up making shoes and tending sheep in the low country of western Leicestershire, not far from the Wales border. He was a big, rugged youth who felt a kinship for all living things and a deep conviction of the unity of all life. While his sheep and cattle grazed, he would sit with his back against a stump and read his Bible. The scriptures had been widely available in English for only a short time, and the new King James version of the Bible (published in 1611) made it possible for all who could read, and could afford it, to have their own copy.

George Fox read his Bible voraciously. But the
more he read, the more confused and discouraged he
became. It seemed to Fox that all the wonderful teachings
of the Bible were somehow having no impact on people's
lives. To most of the ministers and "professors" (persons
professing to be Christians), the word of God was merely a
subject for interminable sermons and theological
arguments. The learned men talked for literally hours
about the fall of Adam and the wickedness of men and
women, while they ignored the love and joy of the
teachings of Christ. It made no sense to George Fox. He
felt a burning desire to understand and experience God, so
he started searching for a spiritual guide.

At the age of nineteen he left his village of Fenny
Drayton and became a wanderer. Going from town to
town, he stopped at churches, called on priests, and often
stayed in the homes of religious people. Everywhere he
went, he discussed the Bible and the questions that burned
in his soul.

"I went to many a priest to look for comfort," he
wrote in his journal, "but found no comfort from them."
After two years, becoming more and more disillusioned,
he returned home.

He continued to ask searching questions of
everyone he met, and some people thought George Fox's
preoccupation with his soul was abnormal. They advised
him to join the army and fight in the civil war. One man
suggested he try tobacco. A priest said he should sing
hymns. His parents and relatives thought he should find a
good girl and settle down. But George was not ready to
settle down. He was looking for God, not a wife.

His spiritual discontent increased, and he went into
deep depression. His health broke down, and life seemed
meaningless. Was there no one who sympathized with or
understood his problem? Was he out of step with the
whole world, or was there a role for him in society? For a

time he even wondered if God Almighty was only a myth—a creature of man's imagination.

Finally, in the black depths of his helplessness and hopelessness, a spark of light appeared. A realization slowly grew in him that God Himself was speaking in the depth of his being. Sometimes he "knew" things he had never learned through rational thought processes. On occasions, a truth would appear vividly in his mind like a flash of lightning. He began to realize, with a deep and indelible conviction, that God always speaks in the hearts of men and women if they will only listen; that God still speaks as clearly in the seventeenth century as He had spoken in the days of the prophets. God was no different. Being infinite, God never changed. Only people changed and drew apart from God. Men and women had shut God out of their hearts, stifling the inner voice, dampening the fire that burns within all.

His life work revealed

One day in 1646, three great truths were revealed to George Fox: that Catholics and Protestants are the same in the eyes of God; that graduating from Oxford or Cambridge is not what makes a minister of Christ; and that the real temple of God is in the heart, not in buildings erected by men. It came to Fox that Christ is alive and well and working within all people. He felt the actual presence of Christ, and he heard His voice say: "My love was always to thee, and thou art in my love." In a deep and ecstatic vision, he saw that "an infinite ocean of light and love flowed over the ocean of darkness. In that I saw the infinite love of God."

Fox started preaching at fairs, in the markets, and anywhere else he could find an audience. He told people they should stop arguing about the Bible, but should sit quietly and listen to God, and allow His power and grace to manifest in their lives. He said the light of Christ was within all, and we should allow that light to shine as a beacon of God's love among men and women.

A group of people gathered around George Fox. Many invited him to their homes, and they told others about him. Here and there, small groups formed and held their own meetings. In the beginning they were known as "Children of the Light."

All his life, George Fox was an "original" and "the copy of no man," in the words of his friend William Penn. So when Fox became a preacher, he was like none other. He opened his mouth only when prompted by God to do so, and he did not believe in preaching at a time or place scheduled by man. He refused to follow any custom or fashion that he felt was meaningless or demeaning. He would not bow or remove his hat in deference to any person or any structure, and he refused to follow accepted patterns of speech.

For example, he insisted on using the terms "thee" and "thou" when speaking to anyone, regardless of rank. This was taken as an insult by most people because, in those days, "thee" and "thou" were used only when speaking to one's family members or to inferiors. As we can well imagine, that habit of Fox's was a constant source of irritation to preachers, magistrates, judges, and other officials who had to deal with George Fox day to day

In 1649, on a Sunday morning in Nottingham, Fox had his first violent clash with the establishment. On approaching a large church, he felt compelled to go inside. After the sermon was over, and the collection plate was being passed around, George got up and told the congregation that they didn't have to listen to those long and tedious sermons. They could listen to God within their own heart, and it wouldn't cost them anything! As one would expect, the minister was upset by both the inter-ruption and the message, and so were some of the other people. While Fox was still talking, officers came in, grabbed him, and took him to jail, where he kept right on preaching. Before he had been there long, he had converted the sheriff, John Reckless, who took his prisoner home with him to meet his family, all of whom became "Children of the Light." Soon after, Fox was released and he continued on his way.

In many of the towns he went through, Fox was "moved to go to the steeple-house" to "declare truth there." And, often, there was physical confrontation. On one occasion, Fox wrote, "The people fell upon me in great rage, struck me down and almost stifled and smothered me; and I was cruelly beaten and bruised by them with their hands, Bibles and sticks. They they haled me out, though I was hardly able to stand, and put me into the stocks; and they brought dog-whips and horse-whips, threatening to whip me." Finally the people "stoned me out of the town for preaching the word of life to them." But, once out of town, he said, "the Lord's power soon healed me again. That day some people were convinced of the Lord's truth and turned to His teaching."

One day Fox went to a conference where ministers, priests, and other "professors" came together to debate. One person would get up and speak, and people would shout questions at him. Soon after Fox arrived, a woman stood up and asked a question, and a minister replied, "I permit not a woman to speak in church."

George Fox jumped to his feet. "Do you call this *place* a church . . . or do you call this mixed multitude a church?"

The minister hesitated, then said, "What do *you* consider a church?"

That was all the invitation Fox needed. He spoke at great length about the church of God being people, not stones, and about the *real* place of worship being within the hearts of men. Finally all the learned ministers, disgusted at being unable to get a word in edgewise, left

the place and went to a nearby inn. Fox followed them
there, still preaching.

In Derby he attended "a great lecture day," and
although, for a change, he politely awaited his turn to
speak, he was arrested as soon as he started talking. After
he told the magistrates that the living Christ resides within
the hearts of all people, he was found guilty of blasphemy
and sentenced to six months in jail.

Citizens gather at the prison to hear Fox speak

While Fox was in prison, many people came to
hear him speak, and some of them became followers.
Even the judges were impressed by the things they heard
of the prisoner, and they allowed him to leave the jail each
day as long as he stayed within a mile. So every day
George walked to the market in Derby and preached of the
living light, then walked back to jail.

Near the end of his sentence, government officials,
seeking soldiers for the civil war, visited George Fox and
offered him a commission as captain in the army. He told
them he would not fight in any war on either side; that
God was love, not hate, and therefore there was no need
nor excuse for war. Angered by his attitude, the officials
ordered the jailer to put Fox into the "dungeon, among the
rogues and felons." There, in a foul and stinking hole without even a bed, Fox spent another six months, finally being
released in 1651.

George Fox was not tamed or pacified by his incar-
ceration—or by later beatings, starvings, and jailings.
After leaving Derby, he went north to Yorkshire, where he
found many new converts. In one area, large communities
of seekers were holding regular meetings. In some of the
groups, people sat in silence, speaking only when moved
to do so by God. These people were known as "waiters,"
because they were waiting for the arrival of a spiritual
leader who would take charge of their movement.

When they heard Fox speak, they were rapt with attention, and literally hundreds at a time joined his movement. Many of them were true mystics and powerful speakers in their own right. They were ready to leave all and follow him, to spread his message far and wide, and, like Fox, to sleep in haystacks or under hedges, accepting whatever God might bring. Like the "little brothers" of St. Francis of Assisi, they felt they had found the joy of the living Christ through George Fox, and they were ready to die for him if necessary.

During this period Fox met a wealthy and influential woman, Margaret Fell, who became a staunch supporter, a dear friend, and, many years later, his wife. Mrs. Fell and her daughters almost immediately became followers, while the master of the manor, Judge Fell, had some reservations. He had great respect for George Fox and his sincerity, however, and he became a strong defender of George's right to speak his views freely. In fact, he permitted huge gatherings of Friends (as they came to be called) to meet at his home, Swarthmore Hall.

Many of the Friends, including the Fells, urged Fox to remain at Swarthmore Hall and continue preaching to the crowds who came to hear him. But Fox was never content to remain long in one place, so he went on his way, following his inner guide.

As support for Fox grew, the resistance also increased. When he went to new areas, local magistrates and ministers sometimes organized campaigns of violence against him. Consequently Fox and his followers were often assaulted with sticks, clubs, pitchforks, and even guns and rapiers. But although Fox was beaten severely many times, he would spring back in an almost miraculous fashion, urging his attackers to strike him again.

One Sunday morning he went into a cathedral and "preached the truth to the people" with such force that many of them trembled and shook in varying states of trance or rapture. (Such states were common among Fox's followers, who became known as Quakers.) Outside the cathedral, he was attacked by a mob and hauled into prison on charges of blasphemy, heresy, and seduction. His friends and followers feared he would be hanged if convicted of blasphemy a second time, so they wrote many letters of support in his behalf. After seven weeks he was released without trial.

An audience with Oliver Cromwell

Now, wherever he went, Fox drew crowds, which worried many high officials. Oliver Cromwell had just been named Lord Protector of the government, and there were fears and rumors of conspiracies and rebellion. An unstable government is always fearful of crowds and charismatic leaders, so Fox was soon arrested on suspicion of plotting to overthrow the government. Taken to London, he had an audience with Cromwell himself, who, impressed by George's openness and sincerity (and not disturbed by George's refusal to remove his hat), asked him many questions about his beliefs and the claims made against him.

"I have heard you are a quarrelsome man," said Cromwell.

"Nay, not I," replied Fox. "Never do I start the quarrels. I only speak the truth."

"The clergy are upset with you."

Fox nodded. "I accuse them of being greedy after money. I say that people do not need ministers and priests; that God's temple is in the heart."

Before the interview was over, Cromwell had tears in his eyes, and he clasped Fox's hands warmly, inviting him to visit at his home. The Lord Protector wrote an order of release for Fox and invited him to a banquet at the palace. Fox declined and said he'd buy his own lunch.

Before leaving London, Fox preached to many

tumultuous crowds and was warmly received. But after leaving the city, he ran into continued opposition. On one occasion he and several of his supporters were riding on horseback through a town when they found themselves surrounded by hundreds of men armed with staves and clubs. By the time they fought their way through the town and to freedom, they were battered and beaten and lucky to be alive. Galloping to a crossroads outside of town, they paused to catch breath, take stock of their injuries, and give thanks for having survived the ordeal.

Suddenly Fox declared that the power of the Lord was upon him and he was going back to face the crowd again. So he and one companion galloped back to town and rode up and down the street, preaching to the people. Although some members of the mob struck half-heartedly at them, most appeared astonished or demoralized, and some stood transfixed, staring at Fox with awe and disbelief.

But in Cornwall, trouble again loomed. The magistrates, determined to have no Quakers in their district, had Fox and his two companions arrested. When Fox asked to see a warrant, an officer held up a mace and said, "This is the warrant." At their arraignment, with still no formal charges filed, the judge asked them to remove their hats, and they refused. Then he ordered them to remove their hats. Fox explained politely that nowhere in the law of England, nor in the Bible, is there authority for requiring a man to take off his hat in a courtroom.

"Take them away," the judge said, his face crimson with anger. "I'll fix him."

All day long the judge kept calling the three men back into the courtroom and ordering them to remove their hats. Each time, they refused. Finally, in exasperation, he fined them for contempt of court and ordered that they be jailed until the fines were paid.

Not only did Fox and his friends refuse to pay the

fine, they refused to pay the jailer for their board, and for
keeping their horses (they had paid this up until the trial).
Now the enraged jailer, whose pay consisted of fees from
prisoners, put them into a horrible dungeon called
Doomsdale, from which few people ever emerged alive.

They survived eight months in that living hell.
Only once were they allowed visitors, when some
religious fanatics came to the prison seeking converts.
These were "Fifth-Monarchy" men, who warned of
doomsday, claiming that Christ was about to return to
establish His reign of one thousand years (the "fifth
monarchy"). But Fox told them calmly that they were
looking in the wrong place for Christ and His kingdom.
"He has already come, and He is with us now," he
explained. "Thou wilt not find Him in the sky. Thou wilt
find Him as a living presence within thy own soul."
Realizing they were no match for the emaciated prisoner
with the penetrating eyes, the visitors left.

During Fox's long ordeal in the dungeon, his
supporters had worked constantly on behalf of the
prisoners, writing letters and begging help from people of
influence. Success finally came after a Friend went to the
Lord Protector and asked to be allowed to take Fox's place
in the dungeon. An official order was sent from Cromwell
to the jail, ordering the release of the prisoners.

As soon as he was free, Fox resumed his travels,
and his meetings drew crowds that sometimes numbered in
the thousands. He went to virtually every city, town, and
hamlet in England, and also to Wales, Scotland, and
Ireland. During the next three years he visited London
several times, seeing Oliver Cromwell on each occasion.
He went to Cromwell's home in Whitehall and urged him
to end religious persecution and to release the many
Friends who had been unjustly imprisoned.

But the worst persecutions were still to come. In
1658 Oliver Cromwell died (two weeks after his last

meeting with George Fox), and the country went through
turmoil and bloodshed for two years. During those sad
days, George Fox had his own turmoil—a long siege of
physical, mental, and spiritual travail and anguish, and
many who knew him thought he would never recover.
Gradually, his strength, enthusiasm and indomitable will
came back, however, and he was ready for the tests that
were still to come.

Quaker movement spreads to New World

In the meantime, the Quaker movement had spread
into the West Indies, and to Rhode Island and
Massachusetts, where the Puritans resisted the "invasion"
by enacting harsh laws. On Boston Common, four
Quakers were hanged, but it did not stem the tide.

In May of 1660, Charles II was crowned king.
Soon after, officers came and arrested George Fox at
Swarthmore Hall. Although they had no warrant, and
none was ever produced, the judge who examined Fox
accused him of fomenting rebellion and being "an enemy
of the king." While he was kept in a dungeon at Lancaster
Castle, Margaret Fell was lodging strong protests in
London. Judge Fell had now died, but his widow devoted
all her resources and energies to the Quakers' cause.
When Fox was put on trial, a message came from the king
saying that "Fox should be set at liberty, seeing that no
accuser came up against him."

During these frightening days, the Quakers were
not the only religious group to be persecuted. The "Fifth
Monarchy" people were causing great commotion and
paranoia, and the king's men were attempting to break up
all their gatherings and imprison the leaders. All churches
that were not affiliated with the Church of England were
disturbed by the Act of Uniformity, passed in 1662, which
compelled all clergy to declare their assent to everything
in the official Book of Common Prayer. Thousands of

ministers who refused to sign were forbidden to preach.

Worst of all, for the Quakers, was the Conventicle
Act, which prohibited any gathering of more than five
people that was not held in conformity with Church of
England doctrines. This law, of course, struck at the very
heart of the Quaker movement. Almost as bad was a
statute imposing fines and imprisonment on persons
refusing to take an oath in a court of law. George Fox and
the Friends held that Christ had forbade swearing, and they
refused to take an oath under any conditions.

Such was the stage set for the wholesale
persecution of Quakers, who ignored the repressive laws
and openly continued to have meetings. Arrested by the
thousands, they were haled before magistrates where they
refused to take an oath, adding another charge. When they
were fined, they refused to pay, so they were committed to
prison.

All over England the police, while trying to enforce
the Conventicle Act, were baffled and stymied. They
would enter a quiet meeting of Friends and demand to
know who was in charge, and no one would answer. The
Friends would continue their meditations. If the
officers arrested all the men, the women would continue
the meeting. If they arrested the women as well, the
children would keep the meeting going. It was difficult to
deal with people who were calm, non-violent, and without
fear in the face of police power tactics.

Nonetheless, the ordeal was extremely trying.
Officers, goaded into violence by their frustrations and the
orders of their superiors, used clubs and fists and guns on
some of the Friends. It is impossible to say how many
died and how many thousands were jailed. During this
terrible period, George Fox endured his longest imprisonment—thirty-three months—much of it in solitary
confinement in a remote castle by the sea. He was
sentenced under the ancient writ of *praemunire facias*,

first decreed by King Edward I in the thirteenth century. Under this writ, a person whose beliefs were inimical to the monarch would forfeit his estate, his freedom, his citizenship, and, if it pleased the king, his life.

Fox survives his longest imprisonment

In 1666, the king released him, broken in body but not in spirit. The cold dampness of his cell, and the lack of exercise, had stiffened and numbed his joints. Walking was difficult, and riding a horse almost impossible. England had also suffered in his absence. The bubonic plague had killed thousands in London, and (on the day before Fox was released) the Great Fire of London gutted the city. Fox said he had earlier seen the fire in a vision.

While his health slowly returned, George Fox toured all of England's counties, receiving warm and enthusiastic acceptance almost everywhere. Then he went to Ireland, where he conducted "large and precious meetings." Returning to England, he was united in matrimony with his dear friend Margaret Fell. She, like Fox, had been a political prisoner, and in fact she was still under the sentence of *praemunire facias*, having been released only temporarily in order to marry George. After the wedding, she returned to prison, while Fox continued his work and made an extended visit to Quaker groups in North America.

On his return to England Fox was joined by his loving wife, who now was free, and they held a series of large and triumphant public meetings. Then George was arrested again and put in prison to await trial. His wife went to see King Charles, who offered a pardon, which Fox refused since a pardon would suggest he had done something wrong. He insisted upon a trial, at which he finally won his freedom after a year in jail.

During his remaining years he spent more and more time with his wife and family at Swarthmore Hall, but he also made many speaking tours of England, and also visited Friends and preached in Holland and Germany. In 1683, when a new wave of arrests came under the Conventicle Act, he attended every large Quaker meeting, practically daring the authorities to arrest him, but he was spared. Finally, in 1688, the king issued a general writ of amnesty for religious prisoners, and many hundreds of Friends were released.

His great work was now nearly done, and his body was frail and feeble. George Fox could still speak with great force, however, and listeners were still overcome by the power of his words and the radiance of his presence. As the end approached, he talked a great deal of the need for the Friends to continue to spread God's message of love and truth.

His final illness lasted three days. According to a contemporary account written by a follower, "He lay in a heavenly frame of mind, and between the hours of nine and ten in the evening of the third day of the week, he quietly departed this life in peace, and sweetly fell asleep in the Lord, whose blessed truth he had lovingly and powerfully preached."

Ramakrishna: Love Incarnate
(1836 - 1886)

In 1836, in a remote village of Bengal, an unusual and precocious child was born to a poor Brahmin family. He was named Gadadhar ("Bearer of the Mace," one of the sobriquets applied to the god Vishnu). In later years he would be known to the world as Ramakrishna, a name compounded from the two Incarnations of Vishnu most beloved by Hindus.

From his earliest days, Gadai, as he was called, was different from most children. Although he was lovable, playful and intelligent, he had little interest in school. In fact, he obstinately refused to learn arithmetic. He was a natural mimic and actor, but he also enjoyed being alone. He seemed independent of everyone, but was strongly drawn to God and spiritual topics.

At the age of six or seven, Gadai first experienced that state known to the yogis as *samadhi*. While walking along the edge of a rice field, eating a handful of rice, he became absorbed by a large black cloud that almost filled the sky. A flock of white cranes flew over, and Gadai, enraptured by their beauty, lost bodily consciousness and fell to the ground. A similar experience occurred a few months later when the boy went to a nearby shrine with several women from his village.

Gadai's parents had few resources and they worried about how their son could ever survive in the world. In those days the caste system pervaded the social structure of India. Brahmins, as members of the priest class, were not permitted to go into business or even to work for wages. By tradition, their lives should be devoted to prayer and renunciation. The only acceptable professions for Brahmins were the priesthood and

teaching; and in those callings they had to subsist on
contributions from those they served.

Even in his teens, Gadai still showed no interest in
pursuing any course of serious study. He had a natural
talent for drawing and molding clay images of deities,
however, and he sang like an angel. He started a theater
group in the village, in which he both acted and directed.

Gadai's brother, Ramkumar (who was old enough
to be his father), ran a small Sanskrit school in Calcutta.
Ramkumar was concerned about Gadai, and he persuaded
him to come to Calcutta to stay with him. He hoped the
sixteen-year-old Gadai would benefit from exposure to the
school and the opportunities in a large city. Gadai had no
interest in living in Calcutta, but he dutifully accepted his
elder brother's guidance.

At about the same time, a wealthy Calcutta woman
known as "the Rani" decided to build a temple dedicated
to the goddess Kali. In India, temples are usually built by
individuals or local groups, and not by religious bodies.
There is no organized religion in the Western sense, and
temples are not places for public worship. Most worship in
India takes place in the home. It is common for people to
visit nearby temples and shrines to pay their respects, and
many go on pilgrimages to tombs of certain saints and
masters. Most temples and shrines are built by wealthy
patrons, who dedicate the structure to their family deity,
hoping thereby to gain favor from God.

The Rani purchased twenty acres of land on the
Ganges River at Dakshineswar, a few miles north of
Calcutta, and set about building a group of temples which
remain today much as they were when Ramakrishna was
there. In the center is an impressive Kali Temple complete
with a portico and courtyard. From the river, leading up to
the Kali Temple, are twelve small shrines to Shiva. (Kali is
considered to be a form of Shiva's *shakti,* or creative force.
The image of Kali in the temple shows her standing over

the recumbent form of Shiva, representing the awakened
Power.) Near the main temple is a smaller one dedicated
to Krishna and Radha, who typify for Hindus the ideal
relationship of the lover and the Divine Beloved.

While the complex was under construction, the
Rani consulted a number of respected Brahmins, including
Ramkumar, about finding a devout and learned priest to
officiate at the Kali Temple. Finally she hired Ramkumar
himself, and he gave up his school, which had fallen on
hard times. Soon after, Gadai joined his elder brother at
Dakshineswar, and he sometimes assisted in the daily
rituals. The Rani was impressed by Gadai, and so was the
Rani's son-in-law Mathur, who managed the compound.
In 1856, when Ramkumar died suddenly while away on a
business trip, Mathur offered the job of temple priest to
Gadai, who was then only twenty.

Intense inner search begins

After his brother died, Gadai lost all interest in the
world around him and began an intense inward search for
God. As he performed the daily *arti* ceremony—in which
he sang hymns and waved burning candles in front of the
image of Kali—he would weep and beg the Holy Mother
to reveal herself. "O Mother, do you really exist?" he
would cry. "Are the scriptures true, or is it only poetry? If
you are real, my Beloved, reveal yourself to me."

Day after day the question—can a human being
actually realize God?—grew in his mind until it became an
obsession. Sometimes he would forget to do the
ceremonies or would lose himself in them and repeat the
same movement for hours. He secluded himself in a
jungle area adjoining the compound, neglecting his duties
and forgetting to eat. His hair grew long and matted, and
snakes would crawl over his body. People would take food
to him and push it into his mouth. Most of the staff at the
compound thought he was crazy, but the Rani would not

listen to such talk. "He is only God-crazy," she said. "Do
not disturb him."

Mathur also believed in Gadai's sincerity, but he
sometimes had his doubts. At one time he entertained the
notion that Gadai's unusual attraction to the goddess Kali
was connected to his lifelong celibacy. So Mathur hired
prostitutes to come to Dakshineswar and seduce Gadai.
After this failed, Mathur actually took Gadai to a brothel
in Calcutta. On being introduced to the women, Gadai saw
only the Holy Mother in them and fell into an ecstatic
trance. The prostitutes, moved to tears, ran from the room,
and Mathur took his charge back to Dakshineswar.

The inner fire

For years, Gadai's body burned with an inner fire
that made his chest flushed and red. His eyes were often
bloodshot, and he reeled and lurched like a drunkard. This
manifestation of heat is well known to yogis as a sign of
spiritual awakening, and the same phenomenon has been
reported by Western mystics. According to the Buddhist,
Hindu, and Sufi traditions, this inner heat is caused by the
awakening of the *kundalini*, or "serpent power." The force
of the kundalini, as it moves up the spine, opens higher
chakras, or centers, producing various physical and
neurological changes.

[Gadai's "drunken" behavior is much like that
exhibited by some spiritual aspirants in a state of "God-
intoxication" or God-absorption. These states are fully
described in Dr. William Donkin's book *The Wayfarers*,
and are discussed at some length in the final chapter.]

Finally, when Gadai's longing reached its peak,
God's grace began to descend. "There was an unbearable
pain in my heart," he later said. "Because I could not get a
vision of Mother . . . I felt as if my heart and mind were
being wrung out. I began to think I should never see
Mother. I was dying of despair. In my agony, I said to

myself, 'What's the use of living this life?' Suddenly my
eyes fell on the sword that hangs in the temple. I decided
to end my life with it, then and there. Like a madman, I
ran to it and seized it. And then, I had a marvelous vision
of the Mother and fell down unconscious . . . And what I
saw was an infinite shoreless sea of light; a sea that was
consciousness. However far and in whatever direction I
looked, I saw shining waves, one after another, coming
towards me. They were raging and storming upon me with
great speed. Very soon they were upon me; they made me
sink down into unknown depths."

The Goddess awakens

After this experience, the Divine Mother was fully
alive for him, and he saw her frequently, both in and out of
the temple, and in various forms. Now some of his
associates, sensing his spiritual greatness, began referring
to him as Ramakrishna. Rama was an ancient Avatar
(Incarnation of God) who was worshipped by Gadai's family, while Krishna (also an early Avatar) was Gadai's ideal-
ized form of the Divine Beloved.

Ramakrishna's unusual behavior continued to
shock many people. Sometimes, inside the Kali Temple,
he conversed or joked with the Holy Mother Kali in a
familiar way. He might lovingly caress the chin of the
statue or go through the motions of dancing with her. He
might take the ritual food intended for goddess Kali and
offer it to a cat, saying, "Here, Mother, this is for you."

One day the Rani happened to be inside the temple
while Ramakrishna was chanting and performing the arti
ceremony. Suddenly, to the shock and dismay of all those
present, Ramakrishna interrupted the ceremony and turned
to the Rani. "You should be ashamed of yourself," he said,
slapping her. "To have such thoughts in the presence of the
Holy Mother!"

The Rani's servants screamed, and her attendants

rushed into the temple to seize the priest, but the Rani was calm. "Leave him alone," she said. "He is carrying out the wishes of the Divine Mother. My mind had drifted and I was worrying about a lawsuit I am involved in. Mother was rightfully offended."

As time went on, Ramakrishna stopped doing the temple ceremonies. He saw the Divine Mother all about him, so considered all rituals to be a waste of time. Often, he seemed unable to distinguish between the Mother and himself, and he would decorate his own body with garlands of flowers and sandalwood, just as he had often decorated the statue of Kali.

His Hanuman phase
In the next phase of his spiritual development, Ramakrishna became the perfect seeker of Rama as epitomized by Hanuman, the monkey hero of the epic poem, the *Ramayana*. "I had to walk like Hanuman," he later recalled. "I had to eat like him, and do every action as he would have done it. I didn't do this of my own accord; it happened of itself. I tied my *dhoti* around my waist to make it look like a tail, and I moved around in jumps. I ate nothing but fruit and roots, and I didn't like them when they were skinned or peeled. I spent a lot of my time in trees; and I kept crying 'Rama!' in a deep voice. My eyes got a restless look, like the eyes of a monkey. And the most marvelous thing was—the lower end of my spine lengthened nearly an inch! Later, when I stopped practicing this kind of devotion, it gradually went back to its normal size."

Shortly after this period, Ramakrishna's mother and his only surviving brother sent a letter begging him to come home for a visit. They had heard disturbing reports about his activities and feared he might be unbalanced or even possessed by an evil spirit.

Ramakrishna returned to his home village for the

first time in years. Soon a local exorcist, hired by his brother, came to see him and attempted to exorcise the entities they assumed were possessing Ramakrishna's body and causing his strange behavior. But the exorcist could find no evidence of possession. The next step by the family was to hire a medium, who seemed to invoke a spirit who announced that Ramakrishna was neither diseased nor possessed. The spirit went on to say that Ramakrishna, being a holy man, should stop chewing betel nut because it would make him lustful. Ramakrishna, who greatly enjoyed chewing betel nut, decided to give it up.

All he needs is a wife?

His mother now decided that what her son needed was a wife, so a search was launched for a suitable girl. Nothing was said to Ramakrishna about these marriage plans. Nevertheless, he told them, while in trance, the name of the village and family where his bride would be found. After the contact was made and all negotiations completed by the families, Ramakrishna was married to a five-year-old child named Saradamani. Following the ceremony, the bride went back to her family while the groom returned to Dakshineswar. (After she grew up, Sarada became a devoted disciple of Ramakrishna. She lived with him for many years, and even shared his bed, but the marriage was never consummated.)

In 1861, when Ramakrishna was twenty-five, the Rani died, naming Mathur as executor of her estate. By this time, Mathur was totally devoted to Ramakrishna, having experienced a vision in which he saw Ramakrishna as both Lord Shiva and the Divine Mother. Now he always referred to Ramakrishna as Father. "Everything here belongs to you, Father," he said. "I am only the steward."

One day a boat pulled in to the ghat below the temples and a beautiful woman wearing the ochre robe of a *sannyasini* came ashore. Known as the Brahmani, she was very learned and an adept at tantric yoga. When she saw Ramakrishna, her eyes filled with tears. "My child," she said, "I have found you at last." She had been directed to him, she said, by the Divine Mother.

From the moment they met, the Brahmani and Ramakrishna experienced a close, loving relationship. She accepted Ramakrishna as an Incarnation of God, but one who did not yet realize his own spiritual greatness. Her destiny was to help him transcend the sex-duality that still veiled him from realization of his true Self. She was many years older than Ramakrishna, and she thought of him as the child Krishna, while he accepted her as Yashoda, mother of Krishna. Soon she began instructing him in tantric yoga.

The philosophy behind the tantras is that the world and its doings are nothing but the divine play of Shiva and his goddess Kundalini. God is in every experience and act, and the aim is to realize Him in everything, including those acts and objects that most people may consider "unspiritual," such as the sexual act itself. By becoming aware of everything as a manifestation of God, the aspirant overcomes the supreme challenge of sex duality.

The tantric approach—using fire to fight fire—is fraught with grave dangers, and few spiritual aspirants have the strength, dedication, and detachment to succeed. In later years Ramakrishna warned his disciples of the dangers of tantric yoga and told them to stay away from it.

During the course of two years, the Brahmani led her student through all the disciplines of the sixty-four principal books of the tantras. In the process, miraculous powers came to Ramakrishna, but he rejected them as soon as they manifested. One result was a kind of celestial beauty that enveloped him. "It was as if a golden light were shining forth from my body," Ramakrishna later said. "People used to stare at me in wonder, so I always kept my body covered with a thick wrapper. *Alas,* I thought to myself, *they're all charmed by this outward beauty of mine, but not one of them wants to see Him who dwells within!* And I prayed to the Divine Mother earnestly, 'Mother, here's your outward beauty. Please take it back and give me inner beauty instead!' And at last that light went in, and the body became pale again."

Falling in love with Krishna

Upon the conclusion of his tantric experience, Ramakrishna followed the Brahmani's guidance in the practice of Vaishnavism as a *sadhana,* or spiritual practice. Based upon love and worship of Vishnu (and the various man-forms in which God incarnates) Vaishnavism is bhakti in its purest form. This is the high road to God, the path of surrender to the Lord of Love, and the acceptance of Him as one's personal Beloved. In this sadhana, Ramakrishna fell head over heels in love with the Lord Krishna, and in spirit became one of Krishna's devoted gopis. He wore a sari, bangles, gold ornaments, and a wig. Those who knew him were astonished at the transforma-tion that took place, for every gesture and movement was that of a woman.

When an advanced soul in the higher stages of divine love assumes the role of the opposite sex, immense psychological factors come into play. By playing the role to perfection, the aspirant can neutralize all gender-based *sanskaras,* or impressions, that force him or her to desire sexual intercourse with the opposite sex. Ultimately, of course, the mind must realize that the true self (the Self) is beyond all distinctions of sex. During this stage of worship, Ramakrishna experienced a blissful vision of Radha, Krishna's dearest beloved. The beautiful Radha approached Ramakrishna and disappeared into his own body. Now he felt the ecstasy and passionate love that Radha had for her Lord, which in turn led to the experience of union between Radha and Krishna within his own being.

Ramakrishna was now almost twenty-nine years
old. All his life, in all his spiritual disciplines, he had
strived to overcome duality through duality—by playing
the role of the lover who begs for union with the Beloved.
Now he was ready to go beyond duality.

Beyond duality to Oneness

Enter Tota Puri, whom Ramakrishna called *Nangta*
(the naked one). Tota was a wandering monk and was said
to be a *Jivanmukta* (a God-realized being who has no duty
in the world, as opposed to a *Sadguru*, who has disciples
for whom he takes responsibility).

Possessing nothing except a pair of tongs (for use
with the sacred fire, or *dhuni*, which he built each night), a
small brass pot, and a piece of cloth, Tota Puri was as
detached and free as a leaf in the wind. As he was beyond
Maya, the world of duality, he was attached to none of the
forms in which God manifests Himself (not even his own
body), and his only devotion was to the impersonal and
unmanifest Brahman. His path to realization had been the
highly intellectual method of discrimination (*jnani* yoga),
by which the mind continuously rejects all that is *not* God
until it accepts and realizes God as the only reality. So
God, in His infinite wisdom, picked a perfect non-dualist
to remove the last veil from the consciousness of the
perfect *bhakta.*

Upon arrival, Tota Puri told Ramakrishna that it
was time for him to be initiated into full knowledge and
experience of Brahman, the formless aspect of God.
Ramakrishna, always innocent and guileless, said he would
first have to obtain permission from the Divine Mother. So
he went to the Kali Temple, to return shortly with the message that the Holy Mother had said, "Go and learn. The
monk came here to teach you."

Tota Puri explained to Ramakrishna that his mind

must discard all attachments. He would have to give up the sacred thread and tuft of hair that mark a Brahmin. He would have to withdraw his mind from all creatures and objects, including his conception of God.

Time after time, under Tota Puri's direction, Ramakrishna went into meditation and tried to still his mind. But each time the form of the Divine Mother appeared in her resplendent glory. It seemed impossible for him to go beyond the form to the formless. So Tota Puri picked up a sharp piece of glass and pierced Ramakrishna's forehead between the eyes. "Now, fix the mind here," he said.

"So I sat down to meditate again," Ramakrishna later recalled. "And as soon as Mother's form appeared, I took my knowledge of non-duality like a sword in my hand, and I cut Mother in two pieces with that sword. As soon as I'd done that, there was nothing relative left in the mind. My spirit soared to the place where there is no second—only the One." Ramakrishna's consciousness merged with the Absolute, and he remained in the state of *Nirvikalpa Samadhi*—experiencing Infinite Bliss, Infinite Knowledge, and Infinite Power—for three days. Finally Tota Puri brought him "down" to awareness of the world while still retaining his God-consciousness.

It was said of Tota Puri that he never stayed in one place for more than three days. However, he stayed with Ramakrishna for eleven months. Then he wandered away, never to return. After Tota left, Ramakrishna went into Nirvikalpa Samadhi for six months, experiencing the unbroken bliss of total union with God. In this state, from which, he later said, few return to the world, the body appears lifeless and needs no sustenance. But since Ramakrishna had a mission to perform, the Divine Mother Herself entered the ocean of his consciousness to call him back to duty.

Henceforth, for the rest of his days, Ramakrishna

never allowed himself to merge completely with the
Absolute for more than brief periods of time. But always
he remained on the edge of infinity, and the simplest thing
—a hymn, a face full of longing, or a story depicting love
for God—would lift him instantly into a state of ecstasy.

Devotees come--and Ramakrishna becomes a Muslim

Now people began to come in great numbers to
see the Perfect Master, Ramakrishna. They came from all
over India—sadhus, yogis, professors, and even a few
politicians. Most were Hindus, but Muslims also came,
and even Christians. Somehow the word got around that an
authentic holy man, a *Sadguru*, lived at Dakshineswar. As
Ramakrishna put it: "When the flower blooms, the bees
come of their own accord." They came to ask questions or
to seek help for problems; they came out of curiosity; or
they came not knowing why. A few came merely to bow
before him or sit quietly in his presence. Sometimes they
went away forever changed.

In 1866 Ramakrishna became very interested in
Mohammed and the religion of Islam. He asked many
questions of a visiting Sufi who impressed the Master by
his supreme devotion to God. To the surprise of everyone
at Dakshineswar, the Master put on Muslim clothing,
asked to have the Koran read to him, and requested
Islamic food. He had become a Muslim aspirant.

Five times a day, Ramakrishna bowed toward
Mecca while chanting the Islamic prayers. He repeated
the name of Allah constantly. After three days of intense
devotions, he saw a radiant figure with a long beard whom
he recognized as the Prophet Mohammed, and who merged
with Ramakrishna's own being.

After Mohammed, Jesus Christ

Some time later, Ramakrishna became fascinated
by stories of Jesus, and he asked a devotee to read to him

passages from the New Testament. One day, while looking
at a painting of Madonna and Child, he was overwhelmed
by love for the baby Jesus and the Mother of Christ. For
days his mind and heart were filled with Christ, and during that period he never once entered the Hindu temples.

One day he was walking alone in a wooded area
when a fair-skinned, handsome man with soulful eyes
approached. A voice in his heart said: "Behold the Living
Christ. It is Jesus Christ, Love Incarnate." Jesus embraced
Ramakrishna and then merged with him.

Thusly did Ramakrishna become an utterly unique
Sadguru. In all the spiritual literature, there is no other
Master who played the role of becoming God-realized
through each of three great religions of the world—
Vedanta, Islam and Christianity—and thereby achieving
the Goal in each.

As time passed, more and more people came to see
Ramakrishna at Dakshineswar. Often he was with them,
talking and answering questions, for eighteen or twenty
hours a day. But the Master kept waiting for the arrival of
his disciples, those close ones he was destined to instruct,
to guide, to enlighten.

"There was no limit," he later explained, "to the
longing I felt at that time. During the day-time, I somehow
managed to control it. The secular talk of the worldly-
minded was galling to me, and I would look wistfully to
the day when my own beloved companions would come.
When, during the evening service, the temples rang with
the sound of bells and conch shells, I would climb to the
roof of the garden house and, writhing in anguish of heart,
cry at the top of my voice:'Come, my children! Oh, where
are you? I cannot bear to live without you.' A mother
never longed so intensely for the sight of her child, nor a
friend for his companions, nor a lover for his sweetheart,
as I longed for them. Oh, it was indescribable! Shortly
after this period of yearning, the devotees began to come."

They were students and professionals—doctors, lawyers, writers, actors, political activists. Most were males in their teens or early twenties, and most were well-read and intellectual. Some were one-pointed in their dedication to God, but some were agnostic, and some were confused and without direction in their lives. In a word, they were like typical young people of today. Yet in a few short years—from 1880 until Ramakrishna's death in 1886—there came to Dakshineswar a group of young men who would carry their master's name and message all over the world. Many of them would later be acknowledged as saints in their own right.

Arrival of Vivekananda

Ramakrishna's best known disciple would be Vivekananda, a spiritual giant who later brought to America the message of the East: of Vedanta, Buddhism, Sufism, yoga, and of the unity of all religions.

Only twelve years before taking America by storm, Vivekananda (then known as Naren) was a youth of eighteen, highly intellectual and a religious skeptic. The first time he went to Dakshineswar, he listened while Ramakrishna spoke to a group of devotees seated around him on the floor. "He looked just like an ordinary man," Vivekananda later said, "with nothing remarkable about him. He used the most simple language, and I thought, 'Can this man be a great teacher?'

"I crept near him and asked him the question I had been asking others all my life: 'Do you believe in God, Sir?'

"'Yes,' he replied.

" 'Can you prove it, Sir?'

" 'Yes.'

" 'How?'

" 'Because I see Him just as I see you here, only much more intensely.'"

That same day, Naren sang for Ramakrishna, and

the master went into ecstasy. Later Ramakrishna told the
youth that he was one of Ramakrishna's long-awaited
"eternal companions." Naren left, shaken and confused,
wondering if Ramakrishna might not be a madman. But
something drew him back; and on his second visit, the
master, with a single touch, raised his consciousness,
briefly, from the world of forms into the formless realms
of light and bliss.

Soon after, the master gave Naren an indescribable
experience—an actual glimpse of God, which removed all
doubts from his mind and made him a lifelong devotee.
Ramakrishna told others that Naren was a great sage from
the past who had voluntarily returned to earth. "On the day
he knows who he really is, he will immediately give up his
body through the power of yoga." (And it is true that the
circumstances surrounding the passing of Vivekananda at
the age of thirty-nine suggest that he may have left his
body voluntarily while fully conscious.)

Ramakrishna's great patience, and the profound
influence he had on people, are demonstrated in the story
of Girish Ghose, a brilliant and erratic playwright.

A recognized genius and the leading light of the
Bengali theatre, Girish Ghose lost his faith in God after his
beloved wife died at the age of thirty. For fifteen years he
was a notorious drunkard, an opium smoker, a patron of
brothels, but still the darling of the Bohemian crowd of
Calcutta. Despite his dissolute habits, Ghose continued to
write and to perform with brilliance. Two of his plays produced during that period ran successfully for more than
five years. All his productions were religious in tone,
dealing with the lives of saints and masters such as
Buddha and Chaitanya. His underlying theme was that
religion is dreary, but men of God are fascinating and
inspirational.

All his life, Ghose had searched for a spiritual
teacher who would measure up to his expectations. So

when he heard that a holy man lived at Dakshineswar, he
went to see him, expecting, as usual, to be disappointed.
He arrived drunk and boisterous. "I've got no use for
God," he told Ramakrishna. "That's why I drink—to show
God what I think about Him."

Ramakrishna grinned impishly and said: "Why not
drink to God? Maybe He drinks too."

Taken aback, Ghose said, "Why would God drink?"

"If He didn't, how would He ever create such a
topsy-turvy world?"

Girish frowned as he digested that; then he asked
Ramakrishna what a guru was good for.

"A guru is like a procurer," said Ramakrishna. "A
procurer arranges for the meeting of a man with a woman.
A guru introduces the seeker to God." The master waved
his hand, dismissing the subject. "You don't need to worry
about gurus. You already have one if you only knew it."

After Girish departed, someone in the room said to
the master, "That man is vile and dissolute. Why do you
put up with him?"

Ramakrishna smiled. "You have no idea. He is a
great lover of God."

Early one morning, after a night on the town,
Ghose arrived at Dakshineswar in a *tonga* (a horse-drawn
carriage). Asking the tongawalla to wait, Ghose went looking for Ramakrishna, who was seated among a group of
his followers. Observing the arrival, the master said to one
of his disciples, "I see he is sober, but he has left a flask
of liquor in the tonga. Go fetch it for me, but don't let
him see you."

Ghose joined the group and sat quietly while the
master answered questions about God and the spiritual
path. Finally Ghose became restless and craved a drink, so
he got up to leave the room. "You don't need to get it," the
master said. "I had it fetched for you. Here. Drink, my son."

Despite his surprise and humiliation, Ghose took

the bottle and drank greedily. But, from that day, he drank
less and less. He continued to come to see Ramakrishna,
but it brought him no peace of mind. He was troubled
about the life he was leading, but at the same time he
abhorred the thought of austerity or discipline. He could
not bring himself to pray. And despite the vulgarity of his
Bohemian friends, he enjoyed their fawning attitude
toward him, and he reveled in the adulation of the theatre
crowd. He was constantly torn between his longing for
God and his desires of the flesh.

One day, in a state of desperation, Girish went to
beg help from Ramakrishna. "I cannot pray and I cannot
meditate," he said. "Suicide would be easier for me. Yet I
can't tolerate the person I am. What can I do?"

"It's simple. Just think of the Lord four times a
day," Ramakrishna said. "Think of Him before each meal
and before going to sleep at night. That will be enough if
you do it wholeheartedly. Can you do that?"

After a long pause, Ghose frowned and shook his
head. "I am an artist. Half the time I don't know when
I'm eating or where I'm sleeping. Besides, I can't tolerate
rules, rituals, or routine. I simply cannot think of God at
any set time. I'm afraid there's no hope for me. It seems
to be impossible."

Give God your power of attorney

Ramakrishna nodded. "In that case," he said, "there
is only one thing to do. You will have to give me your
power of attorney."

"Power of attorney?" Ghose stared at the Master in
bewilderment. "You mean you will represent me? You will
pray in my place? And I won't have to do anything?"

Ramakrishna smiled. "You can stop worrying about
your soul. Leave everything to me. From now on, you
can be a true artist, eating whatever is offered to you,
sleeping where you can, and asking nothing of anyone.

You will have no responsibility of any kind—except you must live by one rule: As thou willest from within me, O God, so shall I do."

"You mean I must be totally resigned to the will of God?"

"Yes. You must live like the dust in the air, free to go wherever the Lord wills it."

Ghose agreed to try, and from that time a great change began to take place in him. He quickly learned that the task he had set for himself was not easy, but the rewards were incalculable. His own ego could never be asserted, only the divine ego of the Lord in his heart. He could not take personal credit for any of his successes or failures. The Lord deserved the credit. Every action, thought, and desire had to be dedicated to God.

Within a few short years, Ghose had not only become transformed, he had also brought about a great transformation in the theatres of Bengal. Traditionally in India (as in Elizabethan England), the stage had belonged exclusively to the male gender. All female roles were played by male actors. Ghose changed all that by bringing women onto the stage. He introduced literally dozens of great female natural talents to the theatre—not only as actresses but as writers and musicians. Where did he find them? In the brothels, of course, where he had spent so much of his time!

So not only did Ramakrishna reform Girish Ghose. In the process he brought about the reformation of countless women who were living lives of degradation and shame. At the same time, dramatic changes were brought about in the theatres of eastern India, which later spread throughout the country.

In such a way does the light emanating from a great Master penetrate into the dark and hidden recesses of the minds of men and women for generations and centuries after his physical life has ended.

Hazrat Babajan of Poona
(1790? - 1931)

On a busy street in Poona (now known as Pune), India, alongside the remains of a gnarled neem tree, is the tomb of a unique female personage. Hazrat Babajan, revered for decades as a Muslim saint, died in 1931 at the extremely advanced age of about *one hundred and forty-one!* Today pilgrims of many faiths—Muslims, Hindus, Christians, Jews, Zoroastrians—come from all over the world to pay their respects at Babajan's tomb, and the number increases every year.

For the shrine of Babajan is not only the resting place of a *Qutub* (Perfect Master). It is also the precise spot where, in 1914, Avatar Meher Baba was spiritually unveiled. Just as John the Baptist unveiled the Christ by baptizing the man Jesus, Babajan lifted the veil from Meher Baba by kissing him on the forehead. With that kiss, Babajan ushered in what millions believe is a new avataric age, which will bring a renaissance of the spirit to exceed anything the world has ever known.

Babajan, according to the best available records, was born about 1790 in mountainous Baluchistan (then part of India and now part of West Pakistan). Her father was a nobleman and chief minister to the emir. As a girl she was called Gulrukh (Rose-face), and she was both beautiful and intelligent. She could recite the entire Koran by memory, and she spoke four languages—Arabic, Persian, Pushtoo, and Urdu. Even as a child she was a spiritual seeker, spending hours each day in silent prayer. (Meher Baba has said that Babajan, in a previous life, was the Persian saint, Rabia of Basra, so it appears she was destined for greatness from her birth.)

Gulrukh was raised in purdah, of course, a strict
system that allowed females few choices in their lives.
She was only about fifteen when her parents arranged a
marriage for her. But the prospect of being a wife and
mother did not appeal to Gulrukh, since she felt herself to
be betrothed to God. When a wedding seemed imminent,
she ran away into the desert. Somehow she wandered,
guided and protected by God, across Afghanistan and
through the Khyber Pass and into the Punjab—across
hundreds of miles of wild and rugged country that was
later immortalized in the books of Rudyard Kipling.

God-realization during the 1820s

After many years of wandering, Gulrukh became
the disciple of a Hindu master, who directed her to live in
solitude in the mountains near Rawalpindi, undergoing
severe austerities, for some seventeen months. Later she
went to the Punjab and lived in Multan. While she was
there, when she was thirty-seven years old, a Muslim
Qutub bestowed the eternal gift of God-realization upon
her. Now, as a Majzoob, drowned in divine bliss and dead
to the world, she wandered back to fulfill her destiny with
her Hindu master at Rawalpindi.

Over the next few years, under the Sadguru's
guidance, she regained full consciousness of the world
while retaining her God-consciousness, and became one of
the five Perfect Masters of the Age. So it would seem that
the amazing Babajan may have functioned as a God-
realized soul in a human body for a full century!

In subsequent years she roamed all over India and
made a pilgrimage to Mecca (while reportedly disguised
as a man) by crossing Afghanistan, Iran, Turkey and
Arabia. After paying her respects to the Kaaba at Mecca
and bowing at the tomb of Mohammed in Medina, she
returned to India by way of Iraq (where she had lived in an
earlier incarnation as Rabia of Basra). Returning to the

Punjab, she moved south to Nasik for a time, then to
Bombay, and finally back to northern India, spreading her
blessings and her bliss wherever she journeyed.

Buried alive in the early 1900s

At the turn of the century, she was living in the
Punjab. She had attracted a large following, and aspirants
came from far and wide to seek her *darshan* (the blessing
of her divine presence). In that region were many Muslim
zealots who lived by their fundamentalist teachings that
God and humans are eternally separate. So when Gulrukh,
while in a state of ecstasy, murmured words expressing her
oneness with God, a group of fanatics (including Baluchi
sepoys of a British army unit) seized the old woman and
buried her alive.

Some months later, the same Baluchis, with their
regiment, were transferred to the military center at Poona,
where they were astounded to see snowy-haired Gulrukh
alive and well and seated under a neem tree in the
Cantonment (military district). The soldiers, accepting the
saint's presence as a miracle, fell at her feet and begged
forgiveness, which was readily granted. Some of the
Baluchis, as well as other local troops, became her devout
disciples. Tales of her returning from the grave, and other
miracles attributed to her, spread across India, and she
became known as Babajan (Father Jan).

Babajan was small but strongly built. Quick and
agile, she walked with her back slightly bent and her
shoulders rounded. According to Meher Baba, "Babajan
had bright eyes, and even at the age of 125 she was
extremely active. She always sat under the tree, rain or
shine. You could feel love flowing freely from her . . .
Always she stroked her left arm. I can't explain why, but
she did it purposely. She used to walk fast, and at eighty-
five would run fast."

Hazrat Babajan's broad face, high cheekbones, and

fair complexion denoted her Pathan ancestry. Her face was heavily wrinkled and perpetually sunburned. She was not known to bathe during the last few decades of her life, yet her skin was always fresh, clean, and sweet-smelling. Her eyes were blue and compelling, and her voice strong and resonant. Her vision and hearing were good. She always went bareheaded, and her luxuriant white hair (which she never brushed) was like a great halo. She wore the Punjabi costume of trousers, a long apron, and a linen scarf draped carelessly around her neck.

Disdaining bodily comforts, Babajan ate sparingly but was very fond of tea. Frequently she walked two miles to Bund Gardens and sat under a huge mango tree by the river. Whenever she appeared on the streets of Poona, people bowed or held their hands together in reverence. Chaiwallas (tea vendors) and fruit-wallas always offered refreshments to her, and when she entered a tea shoppe, people stood in respect. Regardless of the weather, she slept beneath her tree with no cover except burlap cloth. Not even monsoon rains or storms upset her routine.

In a letter published in the *Poona Herald* on February 7, 1967, Major S. Hormusji (Indian Army, retired) wrote: *In August or September, 1907, there was a terrific hurricane in Poona, followed by very heavy rain which lasted for two hours. All the place in the vicinity of Charbaudi was converted into a lake . . . When I went out, I saw Babajan under her favorite neem tree, but there was not a drop of water on her, and the ground around the tree was quite dry. Hundreds of people had gathered to see this miracle. Although it is sixty years now since this occurred, I shall never forget it.*

Many healings and other miraculous events are attributed to Babajan. In April 1903 she left Bombay aboard a ship loaded with pilgrims bound for Jeddah and then overland to Mecca. Far from land, their overloaded vessel, the *S.S. Haidari*, was struck by a violent storm and almost capsized. The ship lost steerageway and rolled helplessly in the towering waves. Panic-stricken pilgrims begged Babajan to save them, and she directed a Bombay man, Noormohmed Pankhawala, to tie a kerchief around his neck and beg a coin from each person on the ship, including the English officers.

Another reported miracle

After this was done and all persons aboard had made a donation, Babajan told Noormohmed to say aloud a prayer: "Oh God, save our ship. With this money we will give a feast to the poor in the holy name of your Prophet Mohammed." According to reports, the storm subsided immediately, the ship righted itself, and the pilgrimage was completed. After visiting Mecca, Babajan went to Medina and, in the name of the Prophet, distributed grain to the poor.

Around 1905 Hazrat Babajan settled in Poona, where she would live for the remaining twenty-six years of her life. Many stories are told of miraculous events connected to her. One morning the driver of a bus going from Mahabaleshwar to Poona saw Babajan plodding along the road near Shivapur, fourteen miles from town. Stopping his bus, he got down and bowed to Babajan, asking her to honor him by accepting a ride on the bus, but she declined. Continuing his run into the city, the bus-walla was astonished to see the white-haired centenarian seated beneath her tree in the midst of a crowd. He got down from his bus again and questioned onlookers, who told him that Babajan had not left her seat all morning.

In 1914, a most momentous event occurred in Babajan's life that will surely make her known throughout the world—the lifting of the veil from the consciousness of Merwan Sheriar Irani, now better known as Avatar Meher Baba.

Lifting the veil from Merwan Irani

Merwan was nineteen at the time, and a student at Deccan College in Poona. Every day, while riding his bicycle to and from school, Merwan passed Babajan's tree. One evening she beckoned to him and he got off his bike and went to her, whereupon she embraced him. Not a word was said, but after that, for many months, Merwan often stopped and sat with Babajan, to whom he felt an unaccountable attraction. Finally, one evening, she kissed him on the forehead, between the eyes, and this kiss lifted him into infinite consciousness—God-realization. (A more complete account of the Avataric unveiling, and the role played by all five Perfect Masters of the time, is given in the last chapter, on the life and teachings of Meher Baba.)

Babajan was famous for her sense of humor. Once an itinerant fakir approached her and salaamed. "For the glory of Allah," he said, "I wish to make a pilgrimage to Baghdad."

"Ah cha." Babajan rocked her head affirmatively and smiled sweetly. "So go, my good man, and may God bless your journey."

"But I have no money, Your Holiness. I have walked many miles to beg your assistance."

"Ah. So you expect me to transport you to Baghdad?"

"Hoy. When I visited the shrine of Khwajasaheb of Ajmer, God gave me a message to come to you. So here I am, and I am ready to depart. Kindly give me sufficient funds to meet my travel and food expenses."

Babajan bade the man be seated, and for the next two days she ignored him. On the third day, a cold morning in winter, the saint was in a playful mood. Beckoning to the impatient fakir, she said, "You want to go to Baghdad? You are in a hurry?"

"Hoy. I have been waiting."

"Chello. I will send you. Stand in the road and be

ready. When I tell you to fly, you are to flap like a bird
and rise into the air. Do you understand?"

He nodded uncertainly and took his position in the
road, holding his elbows out like the wings of a bird. Like
most Indians, he had heard enough tales of saints to be
convinced that Babajan could, indeed, transport him to
Baghdad if she wanted to. But of course, the true masters
do not perform miracles on demand or for show.

After the fakir had stood in the road for a few
seconds, poised for takeoff, Babajan called out "Oorh!"
(Fly!) The man waved his arms vigorously and jumped as
high as he could. "Try harder!" she urged, "Fly, fly!" He
continued his efforts until he sank exhausted to his knees
to the delight of the crowd.

"My dear man," said Babajan, "do you expect to
fly to Baghdad without wings? Come here." He came to
her, chastened, and she said, "Do you want very much to
go to Baghdad?"

"Yes, Your Holiness, for the glory of God."

"How many rupees do you need—to travel third
class with no luxuries?"

He thought. "About three hundred rupees."

"Ah cha." Rolling her eyes upward, she murmured,
"Is there anyone who can help this man make a pilgrimage
to Baghdad?" The hopeful fakir sat back on his heels to
await developments.

A few minutes later a prosperous merchant from
Gujerat approached Babajan and bowed. "God has been
good to me," he said, holding out an envelope. "I wish to
make an offering, dear Babajan."

"I have no need for money," said Babajan.

"But please accept it as a token of my love and
gratitude."

"How much do you have there?"

"Three hundred rupees. Do me the honor of
accepting it."

A murmur swept the crowd, and some of the beggars pressed forward in hope of a handout, but Babajan waved them back. "This is for Baghdad-walla," she said, tossing the envelope to the fakir, who praised Allah time after time as he salaamed and backed away.

One night at the village of Telegaon, twenty miles from Poona, a celebrated musical drama was being staged. The audience filled the theatre and jammed the aisles, and the management locked the doors to prevent others from pushing inside. During the performance, fire broke out in the theatre and the crowd, unable to force the locked doors, stampeded in blind panic. Simultaneously, in Poona, Babajan leapt to her feet and stomped the ground, muttering about a fire and doors being locked, and telling the fire to go out. Persons at the scene of the fire reported that the flames suddenly died down, and the locked doors burst open, allowing the hundreds of trapped people to escape without a single fatality.

In 1921, Babajan's followers obtained permission from the authorities to build a shelter for their beloved saint—a small masonry structure enclosing the trunk of her tree. By then, so many pilgrims were coming to see Babajan that a serious traffic problem had developed at that intersection. The British Cantonment Board asked Babajan to move to another location, but she refused to budge.

Later in the decade, Babajan became less active and walked very little, and now her disciples often took her for automobile rides. Twice she was driven a hundred miles across the Deccan Plateau to Meherabad to visit her beloved Meher Baba (whom she always referred to as "my child"), who had established on Meherabad Hill a spiritual school for boys of all religions and castes.

By the time she reached the reported age of 140, Babajan suffered recurrent bouts with fever. For days she lay ill beneath her tree, refusing to be moved to a hospital.

Her followers made plans to construct a tomb and shrine to house her body after death, and Meher Baba donated four thousand rupees for that purpose. A burial site was sought outside the Cantonment, in accordance with official wishes, but no agreement could be reached on a location. A committee came to discuss the matter with Babajan, but on their approach the old woman flew into a rage. "Get away from here!" she stormed. "I am not going to leave this place."

So Babajan herself ultimately settled the matter. On September 21, 1931, she passed on, and her funeral was the largest the city of Poona had ever known. (Her spiritual son, Meher Baba, was not present, however, having sailed for England and America that very month to begin his mission to the West.) Babajan's shrine was built beneath the neem tree where she had lived for the last few decades of her life.

In the spiritually rich soil of India, great masters and saints have come and gone for countless centuries. Few of us in the West are aware of their names and their importance to humankind. It is only because of Babajan's connection with Meher Baba that we know anything about this unique Qutub who left no writings and very little information about her past. But thanks to her "child," Meher, we have learned a few vital facts about the life and work of a great soul who did God's work on earth for well over a century.

The Avataric Connection

In 1893 Swami Vivekananda went to Chicago to speak at the World Parliament of Religions, and the nation fell at his feet. Dressed in the yellow robe of an itinerant monk, he came to America with very little prior planning or preparation, and he spoke without notes. He had arrived in Chicago with no knowledge of the city, without a place to stay, and he had difficulty finding the place where the World Parliament was being held.

When he stepped to the podium to make the first speech of his life before a large group, there were several thousand in the audience. Remarkably, as soon as he uttered the words, "Sisters and brothers of America!" tumultuous applause broke out and continued for several minutes.

It was a phenomenon that defied any kind of rational explanation. Few, if any, of the people at the Parliament had ever heard of Swami Vivekananda—or of his great master Ramakrishna. But the time was right, the person was right, and the message was right.

In his talks at the Parliament, and throughout his ensuing tour of the United States, Vivekananda displayed an astonishing range of knowledge. He spoke on the following subjects, among others: Christ the Messenger, Women in India, Buddha's Message to the World, the Secret of Work, the Ramayana, the Book of John, the Bhagavad Gita, Bhakti Yoga, Raja Yoga, and Karma Yoga. But the underlying message was always essentially this: All religions are basically the same, and we are about to move into a new age of brotherhood and sisterhood, bringing about a new humanity.

In one of Vivekananda's speeches at Chicago, he said:
> If there is ever to be a universal religion,
> it must be one which will have no location in
> place or time, which will be infinite, like the
> God it will preach, and whose sun will shine
> upon the followers of Krishna and of Christ,
> on saints and sinners alike; which will not be
> Hindu or Buddhist, Christian or Mohammedan,
> but the sum total of all of these . . . [and will]
> find a place for every human being. . . . This
> religion will have no place for persecution or
> intolerance, will recognize divinity in every
> man and woman, and will be centered in aiding
> humanity to realize its own true, divine nature.
>
> Offer such a religion and all the nations
> will follow you. . . . It was reserved for America
> to proclaim to all quarters of the globe that the
> Lord is in every religion.
>
> May He who is the Brahman of the Hindus,
> the Ahuramazda of the Zoroastrians, the Buddha
> of the Buddhists, the Jehovah of the Jews, the
> Father in Heaven of the Christians, give strength
> to you to carry out your noble idea!
>
> The star rose in the East. It traveled
> steadily towards the West, sometimes dimmed
> and sometimes effulgent, till it made a circuit
> of the world. And now it is again rising on the
> very horizon of the East . . . a thousandfold
> more effulgent than it ever was before.

A few months after Vivekananda spoke those
words, a child was born in India who would become
known as Avatar Meher Baba. And now, less than three
decades after his earthly life ended, Meher Baba is already
accepted by millions of people worldwide as the long-
awaited Ancient One, or God-man, the One who came

earlier as Zoroaster, Rama, Buddha, Krishna, Jesus, Mohammed and as other Great Ones throughout the ages.

God has always shown His compassion for the world by taking human form from time to time to guide men and women toward the light of Reality. According to Meher Baba's classic book *God Speaks,* these Divine Incarnations occur at intervals ranging between seven hundred and fourteen hundred years. Descent of the God-man always comes in a period of world crisis, when the release of Truth and divine love from earlier advents has weakened with time. Humanity has fragmented God's message of love and truth into numerous sects, denominations and cults, which compete and quarrel and fight among themselves. Religion is ridiculed, and even those who profess faith may distort God's words for their own selfish purposes. At such a time (as now), the world is starving for a fresh dispensation of divine love and grace.

The God-man always brings the same message

In each Incarnation, the God-man is always the same Ancient One who brings essentially the same message, tailored to suit the needs and conditions of that particular time in history. The God-man's message is simple: Love God and become united with Him.

Jesus said, "Thou shalt love thy God with all thy heart, and with all thy soul, and with all thy mind. This is the first commandment. And the second is like unto it: Thou shalt love thy neighbor as thyself. On these commandments hang all the law and the prophets."

Krishna taught that men and women should live like the lotus, which grows out of the mud and the water but is never soiled or soaked by it. While we live and work in the world, our hearts should always be with God. Work itself should be its own reward. We should be detached from the results of our actions, giving them all,

good and bad, to the Lord. We must take care not to
become like the bee that goes to the honey pot to sip
honey and gets its feet stuck to the pot.

Zarthus introduced "One God" concept

Of all religions in the world today, Zoroastrianism
is the oldest—seven thousand years old, according to
Zoroastrian tradition. [Two thousand years ago, when the
Christ-child was born in Bethlehem, the three wise men
who came from the East to pay homage were Zoroastrian
priests who somehow knew that God was again taking
birth as a human.]

Zoroaster (also known as Zarathustra, or Zarthus)
was the first God-man of whom we have record who
introduced the concept of One God for all humanity. He
taught that we should live truly, think truly and speak truly.
Zoroaster told his followers that he was God's
representative, and he would return again when the world
needed him. (Most Zoroastrians today are still awaiting the
return of their Prophet, just as Jews are still looking for
their Messiah, and Christians are expecting Jesus to
emerge from the clouds.)

Mohammed stressed the spiritual unity of all
people as expressed in this passage from the Koran: "We
believe in God and what He has sent from on high, even as
we believe in that which was sent to Abraham, Ishmael,
Isaac, and Jacob, and to the tribe of Israel; and in like
manner we believe in the revelations vouchsafed to Moses,
to Jesus, and to the prophets by their Lord. We make no
distinction between any of these, and we ourselves are His
faithful disciples."

Meher Baba said, "I have come to sow the seed of
love in your hearts so that in spite of all superficial
diversity which your life in Illusion must experience and
endure, the feeling of Oneness through love is brought

about amongst all nations, creeds, sects and castes of the world."

Most human beings on earth, no matter where or when they are born, grow up exposed to some of the teachings of the God-man. Even though most of us look upon the God-man with the tunnel vision produced by narrow sectarian outlooks, the important thing is that we learn of Him in at least one of the forms in which He walked the earth. That is all that matters. If we surrender to Him, sincerely and wholeheartedly, in whichever form we perceive Him to be, we take the high road to God. This is the path through the heart–the path of Jesus Christ, and of Rabia, and Mirabai, Kabir, Rumi, Francis of Assisi, Teresa of Avila, and all the other great souls whose glowing love for God has illuminated countless hearts and has also, I pray, reflected some of its light onto the pages of this book.

In the final chapter you will read about a man whom a growing number of seekers today accept as the Avatar, or God-man, of this present age.

Meher Baba
(1894 - 1969)

I have come not to teach but to awaken. . . .
I have not come to establish any cult, society or
organization; nor even to establish a new religion.
The religion I shall give teaches the knowledge
of the One behind the many. The book I shall have
people read is the book of the heart that holds
the key to the mystery of life. I shall bring about
a happy blending of the head and heart.
I shall revitalize all religions and cults and
bring them together like beads on one string.

–Meher Baba

It is interesting to note that Meher Baba, who taught that all religions are essentially the same, was raised in the ancient Zoroastrian faith, which is the most exclusive of all the world's religions. There is only one way a person can become a Zoroastrian, and that is to be born as one.

Meher Baba's parents were members of the Parsee community. Parsees are Zoroastrians whose ancestors migrated to India from Iran during the seventh and eighth centuries A.D. to escape persecution by the Muslims. More specifically, Meher Baba's family are Iranis. They bear the surname Irani, which signifies their origin, their religion, and the fact that they (or their ancestors) came to India from Iran *after* the great Parsee wave of the seventh and eighth centuries.

Sheriar Irani, father of the child who would become known as Meher Baba, was born in Iran and was, from early childhood, an ardent spiritual seeker. His father

was caretaker of the Tower of Silence, the place where
Zoroastrians take their dead to be consumed by vultures.
Every day the young boy went with his father to the Tower
of Silence, where he sat and played in the presence of
corpses. In Persia in those days, only the children of
wealthy families could obtain a formal education. A poor
Zoroastrian had no chance to go to school.

At the age of twelve or thirteen, Sheriar left home
and became a wandering dervish whose goal in life was to
attain union with God. After he had roamed over Persia
and India for about eighteen years, an angel appeared and
told him he would not attain Godhood through his own
efforts, but would receive the gift through his son.
Following more years of wandering, Sheriar went to visit
his sister in Poona, India, and she persuaded him to take a
wife and settle down. At the age of 44 he was married to a
young Parsee girl named Shirinbanoo.

Even though Sheriar had no formal education, he
possessed great intuitive wisdom, good business sense,
and was a natural linguist who knew many languages
intimately. (He said he had received the gift of tongues
from God "in a moment," without any kind of effort or
training.) He soon became a successful merchant, a
respected leader in the community, and in time the father
of six children.

The second child (who later became known as
Meher Baba) was Merwan Sheriar Irani, born on February
25, 1894, in Sassoon Hospital in the city of Poona (now
called Pune). As a boy, Merwan was mischievous, lively
and a born leader. His cousin Naja, who grew up two
houses away from Merwan's family, told me that as a
young girl she often woke before dawn hearing Merwan
singing as he walked along the lane. "He had a beautiful
voice," she said. "He wrote songs and poems and was a
natural story-teller. He always liked Charlie Chaplin films,
and he would often get a group of young people together

to put on a play."

In school Merwan was active in clubs and student affairs, and he excelled in sports, especially cricket. He was a good student, but had little interest in mathematics, science, or history. His favorite subject was literature, and he read widely of English poets, including Shakespeare, Wordsworth, Shelley and Keats. His lifelong favorite, however, was the Persian poet Hafiz. Merwan also read adventure and mystery stories. When he was only fifteen, he wrote an adventure story that was published by a London magazine, *The Union Jack*. He wrote poems in six languages—English, Persian, Hindi, Marathi, Gujerati, and Urdu—and some were printed in Indian publications.

At the age of seventeen, Merwan entered Deccan College, in Poona, where he started the Cosmopolitan Club, which was open to students of all races, creeds, and castes. This was thirty-five years before the caste system was abolished in India—and seven years before Gandhi began his great crusade for Indian freedom and equality.

Lifting the veil

In May of 1913, Merwan took to visiting the ancient Muslim holy woman, Hazrat Babajan, who lived under a neem tree near his home. Every afternoon, while returning from school on his bicycle, he stopped to sit with the white-haired lady, whom many in India revered as a saint. One evening in early 1914 Babajan kissed Merwan on the forehead and declared, "This child of mine will create a great sensation in the world and will do immense good to humanity." A few minutes later, Merwan departed and went home, where he immediately went to bed. During the night, he was electrified by great surges of power and bliss, mingled with pain, passing through his body, and he lost consciousness.

The next morning his mother found him lying inert, eyes staring into space. For three days he neither

spoke nor stirred, and for nine months he was hardly aware
of his body or the world around him. His mother, fearful
that Merwan had lost his mind or suffered a stroke, called
in physicians who injected him with morphine and other
drugs, which had absolutely no effect on the youth. One
day in desperation Shirinbanoo stormed down the street to
Babajan's tree and accused the old woman of harming her
child.

"He is not your child," Babajan said softly. "He
belongs to the world. Merwan is destined to be a great
master. He will shake the world."

"But I don't want my son to shake the world,"
Shirinbanoo cried. "I want him to marry and raise a
family." She returned home, sobbing.

Meher Baba later explained that Babajan was one
of the five Perfect Masters (*Sadgurus*) of the age, and her
role was to lift the veil from the Avatar's consciousness,
just as John the Baptist unveiled the Christ by baptizing
the man Jesus. During the next seven years, Merwan
visited the other four Perfect Masters, all of whom were
living in western or central India at that time. Two of them
(Sai Baba and Tajuddin Baba) were Muslims, and two
(Upasni Maharaj and Narayan Maharaj) were Hindus.

Bringing Merwan back to gross consciousness

Upasni Maharaj of Sakori was the Sadguru who
played the leading role in "bringing down" Merwan's
consciousness to the world of forms. After Babajan's kiss,
Merwan had become totally merged in God. The task of
Upasni Maharaj was to bring Merwan back to the world
while still retaining his God-consciousness. The process
was excruciatingly painful to mind and body. Finally, in
1921, Upasni said to him, "You are the *Avatar* (God-man),
and I salute you." Upasni Maharaj directed some of his
own disciples to follow Merwan, and other people, sensing
his spiritual greatness, began to gravitate to him. His early

disciples began calling him Meher Baba, which means "Compassionate Father."

In May 1922, Meher Baba and forty-five followers (Hindus, Muslims, and Zoroastrians, all male) left Poona and hiked over the rugged mountains to Bombay, about a hundred miles away. On arrival, they leased a large house called *Manzil-e-Meem* (the Master's Abode), where Meher Baba established his first ashram. Here, his disciples lived a strict, almost monastic life. Every minute of their day and every detail of their lives was regulated and controlled by Meher Baba, and punishment was swift and severe to those who disobeyed orders. Most of the men worked at jobs away from the ashram, and all their earnings went into a common fund. They rose at four in the morning for a cold bath before prayers and meditation. Each man was required to follow the tenets of his own religion.

After ten months, Baba closed the ashram and sent most of his followers home to await his call. Taking a half-dozen disciples with him, he went by train about two hundred miles east across the Deccan Plateau to the city of Ahmednagar. For most of his life, his work would be centered in and around that area.

On April 23, 1923, Meher Baba and his *mandali* (close disciples) walked down the dusty road to Arangaon Village, five miles from the Ahmednagar train station. They stopped to rest in the shade of a neem tree by a roadside well near the remains of a World War I army camp. Looking about him, Meher Baba remarked that he liked the place and would like to stay there, so the men set about clearing the underbrush and debris from around a long building that had once served as an officers' mess. This was the beginning of the Meherabad ashram, which would prove to be the major center for Meher Baba's future work. On that first visit, however, they remained for only a few days.

Before Meher Baba came to Arangaon, the ancient

walled village was best known for two events, both related
to local saints. Centuries before, in a mosque that is still
there, a saint entered his grave while still alive. More
recently, only a year or so before Meher Baba's arrival,
another Muslim saint had walked along the road and
stopped under a tree by the roadside well. "In a short time
I will drop this body," the saint told his followers. "When
that happens, I want you to bring my body to this spot"—
he marked a place near the road—"and bury it here."

"Here?" one of the disciples asked, "in this God-
forsaken place? Why would you want to be buried here?"

Predicts arrival of great master

The saint smiled. "You cannot imagine what is
going to happen at this place. A great Sadguru will soon
come and establish his headquarters here, and it will
eventually become a large center for pilgrims from all over
the world."

The shrine of that saint, whose name was Gelori
Shah, is there today, near the entrance to the beautiful
Pilgrim Centre, which was built in 1980. Meherabad has
indeed become a place of pilgrimage for thousands of
people from all over the world.

In 1923, however, the land was overgrown with
vines and thorns, and alive with snakes and scorpions. As
soon as the underbrush was cleared and the main building
was repaired and made habitable, Meher Baba announced
that he would soon leave with a few companions for an
extended tour of India and Persia. So his mandali, who had
begun to till the land for farming, hastily boarded up,
packed and departed.

The mandali learned that being a follower of
Meher Baba was exhausting, mentally and physically.
Plans were changed constantly and the most elaborate pro-
jects were often abandoned with little notice. The mandali
never knew whether they would sleep in the open, in the

ruins of an old temple, on a railway platform, in a
dharmasala (rest house), or in a palace. According to an
explanation given by Meher Baba, his work and activities
in the world are only the scaffolding, or framework, of
what he is doing inwardly. His work embraces the
universe, he said, and the results of his work will manifest
over the next seven hundred years, after which time the
God-man will again return to earth. Avataric ages occur at
intervals of approximately seven hundred to fourteen
hundred years, he said.

Meherabad flourishes and the Silence begins

Gradually, during the next few years, the new
ashram, which came to be known as Meherabad
("Flourishing Abode of Meher"), grew and expanded.
Buildings were erected, wells dug, and charitable
enterprises started. The Meher Free Hospital and
Dispensary opened, and special quarters were built for
lepers, and for the homeless and destitute. The Hazrat
Babajan School enrolled two hundred fifty boys and girls
of all castes and creeds. As time went on, more and more
people came for Meher Baba's darshan (the blessing of
being in his presence). On some days literally hundreds of
visitors showed up with the desire to see, join, or obtain
help from the Master. As Ramakrishna said a few decades
earlier, "When the flower blooms, the bees come of their
own accord." No one has to send for them.

In 1925 Meher Baba told his disciples he would
soon cease speaking for an extended period. The silence,
he explained, was necessary because of pressing spiritual
work and impending world crises including wars and other
disasters. On the night of July 9, he gave final instructions
to his disciples. None of them suspected they were hearing
Meher Baba's voice for the last time. The next morning he
rose at five, as usual, and communicated with gestures and
by writing on a slate. Later, he stopped writing and began

communicating by pointing to the letters on an alphabet
board made from a slab of plywood. Most of his many
discourses, messages, and books were dictated in English
on the alphabet board. In 1954 he discarded the alphabet
board and used only his own unique and graceful sign
language, which was interpreted by his mandali.

During the first year of his silence, Meher Baba
spent hours every day writing by hand a book which he
said would be his message to the world and would explain
spiritual secrets never before released to the world. In later
years Baba never revealed the whereabouts of the book,
but he said it was safe and would be published at the
proper time. Today, none of the living members of his
mandali seem to know the whereabouts of the book.

First travels to the West

The decade of the thirties was, for Meher Baba, a
time of extensive world travel for the stated purpose of
making contact with those men and women who would
become his close Western disciples. Between September
1931 and October 1937, he made nine voyages to Europe
and three to the United States. On the first trip, aboard the
steamship *Rajputana*, Mahatma Gandhi was a passenger
also, and he visited Baba's cabin three times to confer with
him. After meeting Meher Baba, Gandhi was inspired to
observe silence for at least one day every week. During the
remainder of Gandhi's life, he had contact with Meher
Baba from time to time.

After three weeks in England and on the continent,
Meher Baba sailed for New York, where he stayed at the
Astor Hotel and then went to Harmon-on-Hudson, where a
home had been donated for his use. Many people came to
meet the "silent Messiah" (as he was described in the New
York Times). They sat quietly in his presence or asked
questions which were answered by one of the mandali who
interpreted Baba's rapidly moving finger on the alphabet

board. Many people, on coming into his presence, wept uncontrollably.

Among Baba's close disciples who first met him during his Western visits of the thirties were: Elizabeth Patterson, Kitty Davy, Margaret Craske, Princess Norina Matchabelli, Countess Nadine Tolstoy, Rano and Nonny Gayley, and Darwin and Jeanne Shaw. Elizabeth and Norina later developed and dedicated to Meher Baba the Meher Spiritual Center at Myrtle Beach, South Carolina.

In 1932, on Baba's second visit to America, he stayed at the home of Mr. and Mrs. Graham Stokes in Greenwich Village, where hundreds came to meet him at a reception. He walked around Greenwich Village and Central Park, and went to movie theaters on Broadway. (When traveling, Meher Baba always seemed to like to mingle in crowds. While the attention of a group was focused on a play or performance, he could work more easily with their consciousness, he explained.)

Next Baba went for the second time to Harmon-on-Hudson, and while there he engineered a contact with a "spiritual agent." He asked to be driven to Sing-Sing, the state prison at nearby Ossining. A disciple drove him there and stopped the car, while Baba covered his head with a shawl for a few minutes. After he removed the shawl, he explained through gestures that he had contacted a spiritual agent who was an inmate of the prison.

In May 1932, while en route to Los Angeles by train, Meher Baba said that he contacted his main agent for North America. Ruano Bogislav, a European disciple, was with Baba when he disembarked from the train during a brief stop at Albuquerque, New Mexico. After writing "Indian" in sign language on his hand, Baba left the station and strode briskly down a street, followed by Ruano and three Eastern disciples. Turning onto a side street, Meher Baba approached two Indians who stood talking together. One Indian walked away and the other—a tall, impressive

man with a red band tied around his forehead—faced
Baba, and the two looked intently into each other's eyes.
No word was spoken. Soon Baba turned abruptly and
walked back to the train. The tall Indian, Meher Baba later
explained, was an advanced soul who served as his principal agent for North America. Each major continent has
one such agent, he said, and these "direct" agents take
orders from the Avatar. Instructions are passed on to
"indirect" agents who in turn utilize "borrowed" agents,
of which there are many. The man in Sing-Sing was a
borrowed agent, he went on to say.

Subsequently, during a visit to Rome, Italy, Meher
Baba pointed out a policeman who was directing traffic
and said that the man was his main agent for all of Europe.
This agent, he said, lived a normal life with his wife and
family, and his wife did not know he was spiritually
advanced.

A message to Hollywood

In 1932, Meher Baba spent six days in Hollywood
(and longer periods on later trips). He was photographed
with Tallulah Bankhead and Virginia Bruce, and also met
Gary Cooper, Tom Mix, Maurice Chevalier, and many
other stars. He liked Marie Dressler's humor but didn't
care for Marlene Dietrich's breezy manner. Greta Garbo
had planned to join Baba and Quentin Tod for dinner at
Tallulah Bankhead's, but Garbo telephoned to say she had
stayed up all the night before drinking champagne and
coffee, and she felt unwell.

At a reception given by Douglas Fairbanks and
Mary Pickford, Meher Baba gave a special message to the
film world, which said in part:

"He who stimulates the imagination of the masses
can move them in any direction he chooses, and there is no
more powerful instrument for stimulating their imagination
than moving pictures . . . . Plays that inspire the viewers

to greater understanding, truer feeling, and better lives need not necessarily have anything to do with so-called religion. Creed, ritual, dogma, the conventional ideas of heaven and hell and sin, are perversions of the truth, and confuse and bewilder rather than clarify and inspire.

"Real spirituality is best portrayed in stories of pure love, of selfless service, of truth realized and applied to the most humble circumstances of our daily lives, raying out into manifold expression, through home and business, school and college, studio and laboratory—evoking everywhere the highest joy, the purest love, the greatest power— producing everywhere a constant symphony of bliss. This is the highest practicality.

"To portray such circumstances on the screen will make people realize that the spiritual life is something to be lived, not talked about, and that it—and it alone—will produce the peace and love and harmony which we seek to establish as the constant of our lives."

Following Meher Baba's three visits to the States in the 1930s, seventeen years would pass before he returned for three more visits in the 1950s. In the interim, some of his close Western disciples, including Elizabeth Patterson, Kitty Davy and Margaret Craske, were allowed to live for years with his Eastern women disciples—including his closest woman disciple Mehera and his sister Mani—at his ashrams in India.

His work with the God-intoxicated

During the 1940s, while the world was caught up in the madness of war, Meher Baba was seeking out a strange and diverse group of advanced souls whom most worldly people would consider to be madness personified. These were known as *masts* (pronounced "musts")—God-intoxicated men and women who, in their inward quest for union with God, had become lost or "stuck" on higher planes of consciousness. Withdrawn from awareness of the physical world, they had tapped fountains of bliss within themselves in which they were trying to drown.

Baba's work with masts is chronicled in the classic book *The Wayfarers*, by Dr. William Donkin, an English physician who devoted most of his life to Baba and accompanied him on many of his "mast hunts." Not only is the book extraordinary and fascinating, it deals with a subject never before described in the annals of spiritual literature.

In India, where most masts live, many people sense their spiritual greatness and are drawn to care for them, and even worship them. Literally thousands of masts live in India, and others, Baba said, are found in Pakistan, Tibet, Arabia, Iran, Iraq and Egypt. There are no masts in Europe or America, Meher Baba explained, although there certainly are mystics, saints, and other spiritually advanced lovers of God. We take that to mean that Western pilgrims of the Path go through the higher planes of consciousness either as *saliks* (retaining full consciousness of the gross world while traversing the higher planes) or "under the veil." For additional information on this topic, see *God Speaks* and other sources listed in the bibliography.

Some masts are so absorbed in their love for God, Meher Baba said, that they require neither food nor drink, nor any creature comforts. In rare cases a mast (or the female equivalent *mastani)* may be so overpowered by experiences of the higher planes that he or she remains immobile, like a lifeless statue, for hours, weeks, or even years. All the needs of masts are provided directly by God. Outwardly, however, they may live in filth (or even eat filth), and their habits may seem disgusting to "normal" people. And while the average person might not be able to distinguish a mast from a lunatic, Meher Baba said that they are poles apart in consciousness. "Mind stopped is God," he said. "Mind working is [normal] man. Mind slowed down is mast. Mind working fast is mad."

Dr. Donkin relates many remarkable and amazing accounts of "mast tours" made with Meher Baba. Near Jaipur, Baba's group found a mast who ate tobacco by the handful. In a wild, uninhabited part of the Western Ghats, they came upon a thin, middle-aged man who stood naked in a field. When asked where he obtained food, he replied that he neither ate food, drank water, nor touched money, but had resigned himself to God.

At Rishikesh, Baba contacted a God-absorbed man who stood every day by the Ganges, holding a bamboo staff and staring at the sun from the time it rose until it sank below the horizon. Near Rawilpindi, in the Himalayas, Baba and his mandali visited a very high mast (between the sixth and seventh planes of higher consciousness, as defined by Baba) sitting naked on a barren hilltop, where he had sat for twenty-five years exposed to snow, rain, and sun. The saint's daily fare, prepared by an attendant, was a paste made of dry bread mixed with crushed stones and wood.

Exactly why Meher Baba devoted so much time and effort to masts is, like much of Baba's work, a deep mystery, but it is clear that the work was a vital part of his mission. He once said that he *had* to contact every mast in the world. Why the physical contact was so important when he presumably maintained constant inner contact was never explained.

Meher Baba often bathed the masts with his own hands and dressed them in clean garments. He took pains to satisfy every whim of a mast, often at great trouble to himself and the mandali, and he treasured and preserved every gift from a mast, no matter how insignificant or trivial it might appear to be. Some masts were seen only briefly, while others were kept in one or more of Baba's seven mast ashrams for weeks, months, and years. Donkin suggests that Meher Baba, while seeing to the creature comforts of God-intoxicated souls, was helping to integrate their consciousness, bringing head and heart in balance and giving them a spiritual push. Even more important, perhaps, he used them as channels for his spiritual work to benefit all humanity.

Mohammed the Mast

A most interesting mast called Mohammed can still be seen at Meherabad, a short distance from the Pilgrim Centre (which houses pilgrims who visit Meherabad from all over the world) and within easy walking distance of Meher Baba's tomb/shrine. Mohammed was first contacted by Baba in 1936. In those days the mast had a prodigious appetite. Each day he demanded, and received, twelve full plates of vegetables, two platters of rice and lentils, twelve bananas, four pounds of boiled beetroot, four ounces of pistachios, and at least six cups of tea.

Nowadays, Mohammed is much less demanding, but his moods are still erratic and he is often oblivious to this world. On occasion he has refused to eat food or drink water for literally weeks on end, and without moving his bowels. Sometimes he smiles a great deal and is affable with visitors. On other occasions he may scowl and say "Jao!" which means to go away. He spends much of his time sitting in the sun on the porch of the original Mandali Hall at Lower Meherabad.

For many years now, Mohammed has been cared for lovingly by an American, Eric Nadel, and his Indian assistants. Meher Baba said that Mohammed is highly evolved spiritually (technically a saint, between the fifth and sixth planes of the mental world) and will be a Perfect Master after two more lifetimes.

While in quest of masts, Meher Baba never revealed his own identity, and his disciples were under orders not to mention Baba's name. (They only told masts that their "elder brother" wished to see them.) Even so, masts often recognized Baba inwardly, as shown by a few of the examples reported by Donkin:

In Simla Meher Baba contacted a mast named Azim Khan Baba, who said to him, "You are Allah. You have brought forth the creation, and once in a thousand years you come down to see the play of what you have created."

On another occasion, Meher Baba approached a mast whose name was Brahmanandi. After bowing and touching Baba's feet, the mast said, "Behold, how my devoted love has drawn the Lord Krishna himself to me."

Once a mastani named Khala Masi was brought to Baba's mast ashram at Jubbulpore. "You are the Ocean," she said. "Give me a few drops of it to drink."

When an unnamed mast was led to the front of a house where Baba was staying, the mast said, "We have come to the garden of Paradise." As soon as Meher Baba appeared in the doorway, the mast cried with joy and ran to embrace Baba. Then, turning to Baba's companions, he said, pointing to Baba, "Look at his face and forehead. They shine like the sun! Can't you tell who he is?"

One day two of Baba's mandali paid their respects to a mast in Quetta, and asked him to come to see their "elder brother." The mast refused, saying, "My boat will drown in that Ocean."

At Bahraich, when a mast saw the approach of Meher Baba, the mast put bells on his ankles and danced ecstatically, singing, "God has come to see me, to give me His darshan."

The New Life

In 1949 Meher Baba shut down the Meherabad ashram, disposed of all the property, and began a period of voluntary "helplessness and hopelessness." Before dawn on the sixteenth of October, Baba and a small group of disciples set out on "The New Life," walking, carrying few provisions, begging for their food and accepting whatever God would provide. Except for those twenty men and women who went with him, all other members of his mandali were sent away to find jobs.

During the New Life wanderings, the mandali were not permitted to treat Meher Baba as the Avatar—nor even as their master—but only as a companion. At the same time, he was the leader of the group, and his orders were to be obeyed implicitly. The companions were under strict orders to remain cheerful at all times, and they were forbidden to display anger or moods. They were not to refer to Baba by name, and were not to imply that he was anything more than their "elder brother," regardless of the circumstances.

Detailed accounts of the New Life would fill many volumes—and several books have already been written about this remarkable period, which lasted about two and one-half years. The tales of the New Life told by Baba's companions are heart-warming, sad, joyous, and beautiful. Some of the unique flavor of the New Life is imparted by a song written in late 1949 by Dr. Ghani Munsiff, Baba's boyhood chum and a New Life companion.

Song of the New Life

Listen to the silent words of Meher Baba.
The life of all lovers of God is in these words.
You who are called to follow the New Life
will renounce your ephemeral existence.

In this life we rely only upon God.
Our will is strengthened by our oath.
We merrily sing the song of hopelessness,
while inviting all pain and calamities.
We neither wail over lost hopes,
nor complain about promises,
nor covet honor, nor shun disgrace.
Back-biting is ended and we have no fears.
This is the tone of our New Life.

No confusion in the mind now,
for we are free of attachments.

Pride, anger, lust and greed are finished.
No religion for any of us,
nor care for mind and body.
The Sheikh and the Brahmin are now the same.
There is for us no small or great;
neither disciple, master, nor Godhood exist.
Brotherhood is the only link,
and our enjoyment of suffering.
This world or the next, hell or heaven,
we are no longer concerned with.
Shaktis and siddhis, spells and miracles,
we are no longer plagued with.
All false impressions have been
purged from the mind;
Now we live with the active present.

Dear ones, take seriously the words of Baba:
Although now I am on the same level with you,
yet all orders from me—good, bad, or indifferent—
you should carry out immediately,
leaving the result to God.
Even if the heavens fall,
do not let go the hand of Truth.

Let despair or disappointment
ravage and destroy the garden of your life.
You beautify it by your contentment
and self-sufficiency.
Even though your heart be cut to bits,
let a smile be on your lips.
Here I divulge to you a truth:
Hidden in your empty hands is treasure untold;
Your beggarly life is the envy of kings.

God exists indeed, and true are the Prophets.
Every cycle has an Avatar,
and every moment a wali.
But for us, it is only hopelessness and helplessness.
How else can I describe to you
what our New Life is?

It would be a mistake to characterize the New Life
merely as a period of wandering and begging, in which
Baba and his mandali subsisted on the fruits of the labor
of others. For it was also a time of discipline, obedience,
surrender, and freedom. During part of the period, the
companions operated a laundry, manufactured and
distributed *ghee* (clarified butter), and ran a medical clinic.
In addition, they distributed large sums of money to poor
and disadvantaged people.

Begging and distributing money in Calcutta

The charitable work came about in 1950, when a
terrible famine struck eastern India and people were dying
like flies. To obtain funds, Meher Baba stepped out of the
New Life for two days and held a general meeting of his
followers, who contributed about thirty thousand rupees
for his work. Then he and a few New Life companions
went to Kali Ghat, on the Ganges north of Calcutta (where
Ramakrishna had spent most of his life).

Meher Baba told his companions he wished to
remain alone in the Kali Ghat dining hall for about two
hours. After permission was obtained (without, of course,
revealing Baba's identity) Baba went alone into the hall,
wearing only a *langoti* (loin cloth), while his companions
remained outside. After a while, Baba clapped his hands
and the others entered. Now Baba donned the special
"New Life dress" (a long white robe and a green turban),
which the others also wore, and they set out begging on
the streets of famine-stricken Calcutta.

It was a scene that only a master could orchestrate. Meher Baba led the way, holding a brass bowl and a cloth bag and gesturing while Eruch Jessawala (Baba's "right-hand man" in his later years) called out, "*Ma, premsay bhiksha dijye!*"—which means, "Mother, give an offering with love." Behind them came another disciple, Pendu, carrying a satchel filled with rupees, throwing coins by the handful into the street, and dispensing money to all who held out their hands.

Baba stopped at each house to beg, and on this day he was ignored or rejected time after time. Finally, at one place, a tiny girl came to the door and said, "Wait, please." Soon an elderly woman appeared and said, "Wait. Don't go. We will cook food for you."

Baba gestured covertly to Eruch, who said, "We have seven people in our party. If you are cooking food, please prepare enough for seven."

"Yes, yes," they said. "We will cook food for all seven in your party. Just wait, please."

When Eruch told this story, he said that the entire family, consisting of the father, mother, children, and grandparents, displayed such generosity and love that Baba was very happy. The family filled the mandali's bags and bowls with chapatis, lentils, green vegetables and fruit, and wished God's blessings on them.

Meher Baba told them, through Eruch, how pleased they were with the gifts, and they departed. That was the end of the begging for that day. They walked to the outskirts of town and sat under a tree while Baba distributed food to all his companions. During ensuing days they distributed money and grain to starving people in famine-decimated villages of Bengal. After that Baba and a few companions went south on a mission to find and help a special class of "truly needy" families. These were people who, formerly prosperous, had somehow lost their wealth and position. Even though they were now destitute, they were too proud to put out their hands to beg.

At Madras, Baba and his companions went into a shop to bargain for a coconut. While the sale was being consummated and a hole was being drilled into the coconut so Baba could drink the milk, a customer was telling a sad story about a prominent man who had lost everything he owned. Prodded by Baba's surreptitious gestures, Eruch asked questions and learned that the man and his family lived about a hundred miles away.

Leaving the shop, they went to the railway station and took a train to the city where the unfortunate family lived. On arrival, Baba and the others remained at the train station while Eruch went to search for the family..

It was during *Divali*, the Festival of Light, and the houses were decorated with lamps and candles—even in the poorest section of town, where Eruch now went. But one tiny hovel had not a single light burning outside, and this was the one Eruch was directed to. As he peered through the open entrance, he saw, in the flickering glow of an oil lamp, a young woman kneeling in prayer before an image of Krishna.

"I was dumbfounded," Eruch said. "No furniture at all; just a lifesize statue of Lord Krishna. It was almost the only possession they had left. I had no heart to disturb the lady's prayers, but Baba was waiting at the station, and I had to follow his orders."

Eruch knocked. The young woman got up and came to the door. "What do you want?" she asked.

Eruch explained that his elder brother, who was waiting at the railway platform, had business to transact with her father. "Is your father here?" he asked.

She opened the door. "Yes, he is here," she said, pointing to huddled forms in a dark corner of the room. Her father and mother lay there, emaciated and ill. "But how does your brother know about my father? And what kind of business could he have with him?"

"He has come to render help. Everything will be made clear. Do not worry, and do not leave the house. Give me your promise that you will wait. I will bring my elder brother here as quickly as possible."

In less than an hour Eruch returned with Baba in a *tonga* (horse-drawn carriage), along with the items Baba required for that particular work. When they entered the house, Eruch carried a bucket of water, a basin, a towel, and an envelope full of money.

Eruch introduced his "elder brother" to the family, but the parents were too sick to respond. Without delay or ceremony, Meher Baba stooped and began washing the man's feet while Eruch held the basin to catch the water. After washing and drying both feet, Baba bent over and touched his forehead to the man's feet, then placed the envelope of money on the man's chest. Eruch told the daughter to take care of the money. Then Baba gestured and Eruch said, "Please accept this amount as a gift from God and oblige us."

At that, Baba turned and started out. But before they could leave, the young woman fell at the feet of the statue of Lord Krishna and cried with joy and gratitude, "Oh, Lord, you are so kind and merciful. As soon as I ask you for help, you send it, my Lord, within a few minutes. Oh, thank you, dear God, for your love and compassion."

"It was a very touching moment," said Eruch. "The beautiful young lady worshipping at the feet of Krishna's statue while in the living presence of the God-man, Lord Krishna himself. Baba was very happy."

To Meher Spiritual Center in South Carolina

Soon after the New Life wanderings ended, Meher Baba made a visit to his "home in the West." A 500-acre tract of virgin forest near Myrtle Beach, South Carolina, had been dedicated to Baba a few years earlier and was called the Meher Spiritual Center. The property extends from U.S. Highway 17 to the Atlantic Ocean, with over a mile of beach frontage and two fresh-water lakes behind the dunes. On a promontory above the larger lake, a communal kitchen and cabins were constructed. Near the north end of the property, on the highest point of land, a brick house was built for Baba. The setting is exquisite, with a lovely view of lake and ocean.

To this idyllic spot Meher Baba came three times: in 1952, 1956, and 1958. On each occasion, followers came from far and near to be with him, and hundreds came to meet him for the first time. In a weathered cypress structure known as "the Barn," Baba met with large groups. Private interviews were held in the tiny "Lagoon Cabin," overlooking the lake and the boathouse.

In early morning Baba often walked a path along the lake to the ocean. Frequently he played ping-pong, charades, and other games. As was typical of Baba, he supervised every detail of the Center's activities, even to planning menus. "I allow vegetarians to follow their own diet and non-vegetarians to eat meat," he said. "I do not interfere with any custom or religion. When faced with love for God, these matters have no value. Love for God means self-denial, mental control, and ego annihilation."

Collision in mid-America

In May of 1952, Meher Baba and a small group of disciples left the Meher Spiritual Center by car, bound for California. As they were leaving, Baba asked Elizabeth Patterson (who was driving Baba in her blue Nash) if she had her insurance policy. Since she did not, they went by her house some miles south of the Center to get her papers. Riding in the car with Baba were three of the Eastern mandali—Mehera, Mani, and Meheru. In a second car driven by Sarosh Irani were Kitty Davy, Rano Gayley, Delia DeLeon, and Dr. Goher Irani.

They drove to Columbia, South Carolina, where

they spent the first night. Proceeding north from Columbia
to Hendersonville, North Carolina, they went west on U.S.
Highway 64 through the lush Blue Ridge and Smoky
Mountains, spending the second night at a tourist home in
Murphy, N.C. The next day, they went through the Ocoee
River Gorge, and Meher Baba said the scenery was the
most beautiful he had seen, and that the area was also rich
spiritually. In Chattanooga, Tennessee, they stopped at
Ruby Falls and Rock City, on Lookout Mountain, where
Baba said they would do their last sightseeing.

In mid-morning on May 24, near a town called
Prague, Oklahoma, a car traveling on the wrong side of the
road collided with the blue Nash. Meher Baba was thrown
out into a ditch and suffered a broken leg, broken arm, and
head injuries. Baba lay on the ground bleeding, fully
conscious, while ambulances came from the Prague Clinic,
seven miles away. Mehera, Elizabeth, and Meheru also
were injured. The other car was driven by a Korean War
veteran, a double amputee, who was driving a specially
equipped car for the first time. Neither he nor his two
passengers were injured.

Dr. Burleson, the surgeon who treated the patients,
later wrote: "I began attending the first one brought in,
who happened to be Mrs. Patterson. By the time I had
determined the major extent of her injuries, they brought
in Mehera Irani . . . Dr. [Goher] Irani began urging me to
come and see about Baba. Of course I had no idea who
Baba was and barely heard her because of my
concentration on what I was doing."

The doctor went on to say, "When I finally got
around to Baba, I was surprised to see an individual so
badly injured still smiling. I was also astounded to find
that he did not speak a word or make any sound denoting
discomfort. I assumed that he could not, but was informed
by Dr. Irani that he did not speak because of a willful act. I
knew we would have to give him a general anesthetic to

set his fractures and suspected he would say something at
that time, but he didn't.

"The most attractive quality of his personality that
first day was the way he would look at me with those big
brown eyes as if he were reading my mind. Later I determined that the most astounding quality was that something
which made it possible for him to receive such profound
devotion and loyalty from so many fine and educated
people. That quality cannot be forced. Such devotion can
only be possible because he deserved it, or earned it."

After thirteen days in the hospital, Baba and the
others returned by car and ambulance to Myrtle Beach. A
message to his followers dictated by Meher Baba read:
"The personal disaster for some years foretold by me has
at last happened . . . It was necessary that it should happen
in America. God willed it so."

(A footnote to the accident takes us back to Meher
Baba's second visit to America in 1932, when he stayed at
Harmon-on-Hudson, in New York. On a morning in late
spring, Baba picked a small pink flower and gave it to
Elizabeth Patterson. Using his alphabet board he spelled
out that she should always keep the flower and should
write down the date. That evening she pasted the flower
inside the cover of her New Testament and wrote: *Baba—
May 24, 1932.* Many years later, after the automobile
accident, she opened the New Testament and, seeing the
date, realized that Baba had given her the flower precisely
twenty years before the crash.)

At a gathering not long after the accident, Baba
was asked the question: "How can the individualized soul
that continuously experiences infinite bliss suffer bodily
ailments and be susceptible to ordinary heat and cold?"

He replied: "It is true that illusory things, one and
all, individual and collective, local and universal, cease to
exist even as illusion when a human being becomes God-
realized, the Perfect One, eternally conscious of his own

infinite Oneness. Whether the gross, subtle and mental bodies of such a Perfect One remain or drop, they do not exist for him—yet he exists for all things within the illusion of ignorance, and his abundantly overflowing Godhood takes care of them, including his body. Until dropped, the physical body of the Perfect One remains immune to ailments, and is unaffected by heat or cold because these are automatically neutralized through his own all-pervading God-consciousness.

"A Perfect One very rarely becomes a Perfect Master, as did St. Francis of Assisi, returning with God-consciousness to the realm of illusion. When he does, he is fully conscious of his physical body and of one and all the spheres of illusory existence, without experiencing a break in the infinite bliss of the indivisible Oneness of his being.

"In short, the God-realized or Perfect One has God-consciousness with no consciousness whatever of anything else, as nothing other than God exists for him." However, Baba said, "The Perfect Master has God-consciousness plus consciousness of illusion.

"It is the complete and absolute unconsciousness of his body (as of all other illusory things) that keeps the body of the Perfect One untouched by environmental conditions and effects, whereas it is the regaining of consciousness of the body which makes the Perfect Master susceptible to its ordinary ailments and sufferings.

"Not only do Perfect Masters not use their divine power to avoid or alleviate their own physical suffering which they consciously experience as illusion, but they take upon themselves physical suffering in order to alleviate the spiritual ignorance of others who are in the bondage of illusion. St. Francis of Assisi suffered such excruciating headaches that he had to dash his head against stone, although others could be healed by the touch of his hand."

Continuing, Meher Baba said, "Jesus Christ suffered the tortures of crucifixion to take on the suffering of the universe. Being simultaneously the Father and Son, His own infinite bliss was not interrupted by the cross, nor did this status intervene in the bodily agony which He suffered as an ordinary human being. The sublime difference in individual suffering lies in the fact that an ordinary man suffers for himself, Masters suffer for humanity, and the Avatar suffers for one and all beings and things."

Last visits to America

In July of 1956, Meher Baba left India with four of his male mandali on a whirlwind world tour. After stopping at Zurich, Paris, and London, they flew to New York and stayed four days at the Hotel Delmonico. Then, accompanied by fifty of Baba's American "lovers" (a term Baba used in preference to the traditional "devotees"), he flew to Wilmington, North Carolina, and was driven to the Meher Spiritual Center for a six-day *sahavas* (intimate gathering of Master and disciples).

Leaving Myrtle Beach, he flew to Washington, D.C., for a one-day stay, then on to Los Angeles. He and his party drove to Meher Mount, near Ojai, where a lovely site had been dedicated to him. Later they visited San Francisco and went to Muir Woods, where Baba was photographed sitting in the hollow of a huge redwood tree. On August 7 he flew to Sydney, Australia, and stayed at Meher House, which had been built for him by his close disciples Francis Brabazon and Bill LePage.

His last visit to the United States was in 1958. With three male disciples, he arrived in New York on May 17 and went directly to Myrtle Beach, where a sahavas program for several hundred of his lovers was held at the Barn. (He was convalescing from injuries suffered in a second automobile accident, which occurred in India in 1956, and he was carried about the Center in a special

chair.) He also officiated at a "birthday" party for forty
children. Several musical programs were held, featuring
both Eastern *qwaalis* and Western music (including "Begin
the Beguine," which Baba said had eternal significance,
and which he arranged to have played at his tomb after he
passed on). One performance was put on for him by
dancers brought by Margaret Craske, a long-time disciple
who was an author and well-known ballet teacher in both
London and New York. Leaving Myrtle Beach, he flew to
Australia for the dedication of a lovely retreat in Queensland
known as Avatar's Abode.

Before Meher Baba had left the Meher Spiritual
Center on May 30, he told Elizabeth Patterson that many
more people in the future might visit the Center—even
when he was not physically there. She asked him who
should be permitted to visit, and he said, "Those who love
and follow me, and those who know of me and want to
know more."

Over the succeeding years, Meher Baba's wishes
have been followed carefully—by Mrs. Patterson (who
passed on in 1980); by Kitty Davy, who died in 1991 at the
age of one hundred; and by Jane Barry Haynes, who
passed away in 1997. Currently the Center, a non-profit
foundation, is managed by a board of directors with a full-
time executive director, Barbara Plews. The retreat is open
throughout the year (both for day visitors and persons
staying overnight in the cabins), and visitors come from
all over the world. This is also true of Avatar's Abode in
Australia.

During the 1960s Meher Baba spent a great deal of
time in seclusion, preoccupied with his "universal work,"
but in 1962 he held an "East-West Gathering" in Poona.
About 3,500 of his lovers from all over the world came to
see their master for what turned out to be the last time for
most of them. The gathering took place at Guruprasad, the
magnificent home and gardens of the Maharani of Baroda,

a devoted follower of Baba. The sahavas coincided with two world crises—the invasion of India by China, and the Cuban missile confrontation between Russia and the United States.

During his welcoming message, Baba said, through Eruch: "All religions of the world proclaim that there is but one God, the Father of all in creation. I am that Father. I have come to remind all people that they should live on earth as the children of the one Father until my grace awakens them to the realization . . . that all divisions and conflicts and hatred are but a shadow play of their own ignorance.

"Although all are my children, they ignore the simplicity and beauty of this Truth by indulging in hatred, conflicts and wars that divide them in enmity, instead of living as one family in their Father's house. . . . It is time that they become aware of the presence of their Father in their midst and of their responsibility towards Him and themselves . . ."

In other messages given during the gathering, Baba spoke of evolution, involution, and God-realization, explaining that everything and everyone in creation is destined for the same Goal of union (or "reunion," we should say) with God. He said that throughout millions of galaxies, life forms have evolved on innumerable planets. On some of them, evolution is complete, and human beings exist. However, even though people on some other planets are highly developed intellectually, only on Earth can the head and heart attain perfect balance so that God can be realized. Consequently all souls in other worlds must reincarnate on Earth before they can enter the Spiritual Path.

Near the end of 1968 Baba announced that his work had been completed—to his 100% satisfaction—and the results would manifest in due time. On January 31, 1969, at 12:15 p.m., he left his physical form, and his

body was taken to Meherabad Hill. For the next seven days
and nights, as the body lay in a bed of flowers, tens
of thousands of worshippers paid their respects at the tomb
Baba had built decades before, and which bears the
symbols of the world's major religions.

During those seven days, another remarkable and
unprecedented event was taking place thousands of miles
away in Arabia. In the holy city of Mecca, the sacred
Kaaba, toward which Muslims all over the world bow five
times a day, was submerged by flood waters for the first
time in history. According to accounts published in
newspapers in India, Pakistan and other Islamic countries,
the Kaaba was under two meters of water and inaccessible
to worshippers from January 31 until February 7, 1969.
[At about the same time, the cultural and financial center
of the western world, New York City, was brought to its
knees by a devastating electrical blackout!]

To mystics throughout the world, the simultaneity
of these events has great meaning. To some it signifies the
passing of the avataric mantle from Mohammed the
Prophet to Avatar Meher Baba. From this point of view,
the age of Mohammed has ended and the age of Meher
Baba has begun.

This is not to say that Islam is no longer a valid
and effective approach to God, any more than to say that
the Christian era ended when Islam swept like wildfire
across the Middle East. It is only to suggest that God in
His infinite compassion has given to humanity a new and
fresh gift of His love, beauty, and perfection crystallized in
a man-form for humankind to study, compare, ponder, and
to weigh; for some to ignore, fear, revile, or hate; for
others to accept, embrace, love, and to follow.

Did Meher Baba break his silence?

Baba's silence was one of the great mysteries of his
life. From almost the time he began it, he promised to

break his silence in the near future. The breaking of his silence, he said, would signal the dawn of a great world-wide spiritual awakening. Often he set actual dates for the breaking of his silence, and these were always postponed or re-set. It seems clear that he wanted his followers to continually expect a breaking of his silence.

And when he broke his silence, he said, it would not be for the purpose of delivering lectures, messages or discourses. He would say only one word, and this word would go to the heart of all beings in creation.

In some of his messages he stressed that the one word he would utter would be that Original Word of God that brought the world and all life into existence. He explained that the Primal Oceanic Sound emerging through the "Om-point" produced the Mental Sphere (the domain of mind), the Subtle Sphere (the domain of energy) and the Gross Sphere (domain of matter). So when he, the Avatar, broke his silence, it would result in a universal expansion of consciousness that would raise humankind from the Age of Reason to the Age of Intuition.

Several decades have passed since Meher Baba's body was laid to rest in 1969. Already we have seen dramatic changes in human consciousness. And this, he has promised us, is only the beginning.

So did Meher Baba break his silence?

We can only answer, "God only knows."

My opinion, however, is that he did break his silence, but obviously not in the way that many people thought he would break it. Otherwise, what would induce thousands of people who never saw Meher Baba to travel halfway around the world to India to visit the places where he lived and worked, and to spend long hours at the small, domed building on Meherabad Hill where his remains are interred?

If Meher Baba was and is *not* the Avatar, who on earth could he have been? Was he a fraud? Was he crazy or deluded?

Meher Baba was celibate all his life. ("Sex for me does not exist," he said.) For most of his life he never touched money except when giving it to the poor. As far as I have been able to learn, virtually everyone who ever met him considered him to stand out beyond anyone else they had ever seen or met. If he was not the Ancient One, as he claimed to be, who was he? What was his motive?

What did he get out of working with lepers, with the God-intoxicated, with fasting for long periods, with observing silence for most of his life?

And if he *was* the Avatar, the same God-man who came as Zoroaster, Jesus, Krishna, Rama, Buddha and Mohammed, we must take him seriously. It doesn't matter who you are, where you've been and what you've done, he tells us. We're all on the same treadmill, and there's an easy way to get off. All we have to do, he says, is "Love God, and become God."

During his forty-four years of silence, he gave many hints of what is to come. He said: "When an atom is split, an infinite amount of energy is released. Similarly, when my silence is broken and I utter the Word, infinite wisdom will be released. . . .When an atom bomb strikes the earth, it causes vast devastation. Similarly, when the Word that I utter strikes the universe, there will be great material destruction, but there will also be a tremendous spiritual upheaval."

Many people feel that the world is now beginning to experience some of the early results of the breaking of Meher Baba's silence. If they are right, these effects will accelerate as time goes on. Hang on! It's going to be a wonderful ride!

Bibliography and Recommended Reading

Adriel, Jean. Avatar. Santa Barbara, CA: J.F. Rowny Press, 1947.

Anzar, Naosherwan. (Editor). The Ancient One. (Memoirs of Meher Baba by Eruch Jessawala.) Ahmednagar, MS, India: Avatar Meher Baba Perpetual Public Charitable Trust, 1985.

Anzar, Naosherwan. Glow International, a Journal Devoted to Meher Baba. Beloved Books: P.O. Box 10, New York, NY 10185.

Anzar, Naosherwan. Presence. New York: Beloved Books, 1991.

Anzar, Naosherwan. The Beloved. Myrtle Beach, SC: Sheriar Press, 1974.

Arberry, A.J. (editor and translator). Fifty Poems of Hafiz. London: Cambridge University Press, 1953.

Attar, Farid al-Din. Muslim Saints and Mystics. Translated by A.J. Arberry. London: Routledge & Kegan Paul Ltd., 1966.

The Awakener (a journal devoted to Meher Baba, edited and published for many years by Filis Frederick). Universal Spiritual League in America, Inc.

Barks, Coleman. The Essential Rumi. San Francisco: Harper San Francisco, 1995.

Bjerragaard, C.H.A. Mysticism. New York: Knight and Brown, 1902.

Bly, Robert (editor), The Kabir Book. Boston: Beacon Press, 1977.

Brabazon, Francis. Stay With God. Melbourne, Australia: New Humanity Books, 1990.

Brabazon, Francis. The Beloved Is All in All. New York: Beloved Books.

Craske, Margaret. The Dance of Love: My Life with Meher Baba. Myrtle Beach, SC: Sheriar Press, 1980.

Craske, Margaret. Still Dancing with Love: More Stories of Life with Meher Baba. Myrtle Beach, SC: Sheriar Press, 1990.

Dadachanji, Arnavaz N. Gift of God. New York: Beloved Books, 1995.

Davy, Kitty. Love Alone Prevails. Myrtle Beach, SC: Sheriar Press, 1981.

DeLeon, Delia. The Ocean of Love: My Life with Meher Baba. Myrtle Beach, SC: Sheriar Press, 1991.

Donkin, William. The Wayfarers. Myrtle Beach, SC: Sheriar Press, 1988.

Eaton, Bili. A Love So Amazing: Memories of Meher Baba. Myrtle Beach, SC: Sheriar Press, 1983.

Evans-Wentz, W.Y. (editor). Tibet's Great Yogi Milarepa. London: Oxford University Press, 1969.

Fremantle, Anne. The Protestant Mystics. New York: Little, Brown, 1964.

French, R.M. (translator). The Way of a Pilgrim. New York: Ballantine Books, 1974.

Gayley, Rano. Because of Love: My Life and Art with Meher Baba. Myrtle Beach, SC: Sheriar Press, 1983.

Green, Julien. God's Fool: The Life and Times of Francis of Assisi. Harper San Francisco, 1987.

Haynes, Jane Barry. Letters of Love for Meher Baba. Myrtle Beach, SC: EliNor Publications, 1997.

Haynes, Jane Barry (Editor). Treasures from the Meher Baba Journals. Myrtle Beach, SC: Sheriar Press, 1979.

Hopkinson, Tom and Dorothy. Much Silence. New York: Dodd, Mead, 1975.

Irani, Mani S. God-Brother: Stories of My Childhood with Meher Baba. Myrtle Beach, SC, Sheriar Foundation, 1993.

Irani, Mehera. Mehera (the Life Story of Mehera J. Irani). New York: Beloved Books, 1989.

James, William. The Varieties of Religious Experience. New York: Collier Books, 1972.

Jessawala, Eruch. That's How It Was: Stories of Life with Meher Baba. Myrtle Beach, SC: Sheriar Foundation, 1995.

Jones, Rufus M. The Story of George Fox. Philadelphia: Friends Book Store, 1943.

Kalchuri, Bhau. Lord Meher (a multi-volume biography of Meher Baba). Asheville, NC: Manifestation, Inc.
Ladinsky, Daniel. I Heard God Laughing: Renderings of Hafiz. Walnut Creek, CA: Sufism Reoriented, 1996.

Ladinsky, Daniel. The Subject Tonight Is Love: 60 Wild and Sweet Poems of Hafiz. Myrtle Beach, SC: Pumpkin House Press, 1996.

Brother Lawrence. The Practice of the Presence of God. Mount Vernon, NY: Peter Pauper Press, 1963.

Le Page, Bill. The Turning of the Key: Meher Baba in Australia. Myrtle Beach, SC: Sheriar Press, 1993.

Le Page, Bill. (Editor). It So Happened: Stories from Days with Meher Baba. Balmain, NSW, Australia: Meher Baba Foundation, 1978.

Le Page, Bill. Not We But One: Meher Baba on Life, Living and Love. Balmain, NSW, Australia: Meher Baba Foundation, 1977.

Love Street LampPost, a quarterly published by the Avatar Meher Baba Center of Southern California, 1214 South Van Ness Avenue, Los Angeles, CA 90019-3520.

Matchabelli, Princess Norina. Norina's Gift: Messages from Meher Baba. Introduction by Christopher Wilson and Charles Haynes. Myrtle Beach, SC: EliNor Publications, 1997.

Meher Baba. Discourses. Myrtle Beach, SC: Sheriar Press, 1987.

Meher Baba. God Speaks. New York: Dodd, Mead & Co., 1973.

Meher Baba. The Everything and the Nothing. Myrtle Beach, SC: Sheriar Press, 1995.

Meher Baba. Life at Its Best. Walnut Creek, CA: Sufism Reoriented, 1974.

Meher Baba. Listen Humanity. Narrated and edited by D. E. Stevens. Monaco: Companion Books, 1985.

Mukerji, Dhan Gopal. The Face of Silence (a biography of Ramakrishna). New York: E.P. Dutton, 1926.

Natu, Bal. Glimpses of the God-Man, Meher Baba. Six volumes to date. Myrtle Beach, SC: Sheriar Foundation.

Natu, Bal. Conversations with the Awakener. Myrtle Beach, SC: Sheriar Foundation, 1991.

Natu, Bal. More Conversations with the Awakener. Myrtle Beach, SC: Sheriar Foundation, 1993.

Natu, Bal. The Samadhi, Star of Infinity: The Tomb-Shrine of Avatar Meher Baba. Myrtle Beach, SC: Sheriar Foundation, 1997.

Nicholson, Reynolds A. The Mystics of Islam. London: Routledge & Kegan Paul, 1975.

Nicholson, Reynolds A. (Editor and translator.) Rumi: Divani Shamsi Tabriz. San Francisco: The Rainbow Bridge, 1973.

Nikhilanda, Swami (translator). The Gospel of Sri Ramakrishna. New York: Ramakrishna-Vivekananda Center, 1942.

Pennington, M. Basil. Centering Prayer. New York: Doubleday, 1980.

Purdom, Charles B. God to Man and Man to God. Myrtle Beach, SC: Sheriar Press, 1975.

Purdom, Charles B. The God-Man. Myrtle Beach, SC: 1971.

Purdom, Charles B. The Perfect Master. London: Williams and Norgate, 1937.

Saradananda, Swami. Ramakrishna the Great Master. Madras, India: Ramakrishna Math, 1979.

Sethi, V.K. Kabir: the Weaver of God's Name. Punjab, India: Radha Soami Satsang Beas, 1984.

Smith, Margaret. Rabia the Mystic and Her Fellow Saints in Islam. Amsterdam: Philo Press, 1928.

Smith, Paul. Divan of Hafiz (two volumes). Melbourne, Australia: New Humanity Books, 1983.

Stephens, William M. Footprints in the Sand. Nashville: Oceanic Press, 1997.

Stevens, Don E. Listen! The New Humanity. New York: Beloved Books, 1990.

Tagore, Rabindranath. Songs of Kabir. New York: Samuel Weiser, 1989.

Teresa: The Life of St. Teresa of Jesus. Westminster, MD: Newman Press, 1951.

Underhill, Evelyn. The Mystics of the Church. New York: Schockken Books, 1964.

Vedanta Society. Women Saints, East and West. Hollywood, CA: Vedanta Press, 1955.

Vivekananda, Swami. The Yogas and Other Works. New York: Ramakrishna-Vivekananda Center, 1953.

Yolen, Jane. The Story of George Fox and the Quakers. New York: The Seabury Press, 1972.

206

Index

Some comments on another Oceanic Press book by William M. Stephens:

"...a superb 'page-turner'– I was enthralled, inspired and tickled by the range of potent poetic images, intimate and fascinating life details, and real insights into the nature, direction and synchronicities of the spiritual path. *Footprints* fills a significant niche." —Allan Y. Cohen, Ph.D., author of *Mastery of Consciousness*; co-author of *Understanding Drug Use: an Adult's Guide to Drugs and the Young.*

"*Footprints in the Sand* is brimful of God's presence. It weaves His shining light between the sentences, dancing with the words. It had me on the edge of my seat, waiting to see the outcome of some of the real-life vignettes. ... Thank you for sharing this part of His stream of Love. —Jeanne Taylor, Fort Campbell, KY.

"My hat is off to you; clear and concise writing style, no-flourish treatment and *interesting* stories. Thank God for the teller who knows what in his life *is* interesting." —Beth McKee, Myrtle Beach, S.C.

Footprints in the Sand is a memoir of the author's life from the time, in 1969, when he went through a near-death experience and discovered a world of light, love and beauty he hadn't known existed. The experience changed him from an agnostic to a spiritual seeker, and also erased his addiction to drugs and alcohol. He and his wife Peggy became followers of Avatar Meher Baba and made a pilgrimage to Meher Baba's home in India. The book contains inspiring stories, anecdotes, poems and photographs of Meher Baba's disciples and followers. Paperback, 144 pages, $12.

Footprints in the Sand and *Souls on Fire* are sold by leading bookstores as well as online. If your bookstore does not stock copies, you may order direct from the publisher at $12 per book plus $3 for shipping and handling. (A single shipping charge of $3 will cover shipping costs for as many as three books in any combination.) Tennessee residents please add 6% sales tax. Your check should accompany your order. Sorry – we don't accept credit cards.

Oceanic Press
P. O. Box 3705
Brentwood, TN 37024-3705
Phone: 615-373-9843
Fax: 615-370-8963

William M. Stephens was born in Chattanooga. He and his wife Peggy met in high school. On his seventeenth birthday, after Pearl Harbor was attacked, Stephens joined the U. S. Marine Corps and served in the Central Pacific. Later he received degrees in law and marine science. He practiced law for many years, worked in marine science, and also taught college courses in law, criminal justice and creative writing. A pioneer Scuba-diver and underwater photographer, he survived a frightening adventure in 1959 when his diving gear malfunctioned at a depth of 200 feet during an archaeological excavation.

After a near-death experience in 1969, Stephens made a pilgrimage to India, became a follower of Avatar Meher Baba and began writing about saints and mystics and the joys of following a God-realized Master.